We are self-taught in the matter of using our time. As soon as we start school we are given a watch and a schedule. Our initiation has begun.

Soon afterward our in-basket, which is made of only twenty-four hours, starts to fill up: commutes, meetings, work, appointments, sleep, telephone calls, e-mails by the dozens, meals, sports, shopping, love life, newspapers, babies to feed, notes to compile, errands—and—darn it! It's Christmas and I still haven't bought any gifts!

Some people fall apart, others organize themselves. Most hurt for time and do not know that the illness can be cured. It is for them that I write this book.

We have been told that time is money; but it is really life, our life. We cannot accept the stress and the discomfort that undermine both our effectiveness and our pleasure in life.

In the twentieth century we made many drastic changes: in our health, material well-being, speed, communication, space, and now in our bodies. It is clear that now our next conquest must be time. This conquest will not be easy as it is a bare-knuckled fight with ourselves, but it is worthwhile because it makes life more serene and may lead to wisdom.

You Waste Your Time

What is time? · *Time is our transformation*
· *The most democratic of our resources* · *We all have the same room* · *Technology is a source of stress* · *The nature of modern time* · *How stress was born* · *The march toward a unique time* · *Free time is shrinking* · *Can we take our time?*· *We choose the moment* · *Time is money* · *Jet lag* · *The ecology of time*

What is time?

THE FIRST paradox of time is this: It is so crucial for us humans that we all wear on our wrist the instrument that proclaims its sovereignty. However, specialists, such as philosophers, continue to ponder its nature, and sometimes even question its existence. When they speak, they generally begin by hiding behind St. Augustine's famous statement: "What is time? If no one asks me, I know what it is; but if someone asks and I must explain, I no longer know what it is."

Nevertheless, the rug in the living room wears out, the coffee gets cold, I, again, need to get my hair cut—and all this is measured in minutes, weeks, or years.

Scientists even study the "arrow of time," a theoretical notion which posits that time is reversible. Physicists think time can be reversed, but can an omelet revert to being a dozen eggs? They admit that time is not reversible in the case of the omelet but claim that the theory works for certain almost imperceptible particles.

But the age of our arteries is perceptible, and it always catches up to us. "My mission is to kill time and time's mission is to kill me. Assassins feel at ease with each other," said E. M. Cioran.

What would it feel like if the universe freezes suddenly, like a frame in a video. *If nothing moves or evolves, time disappears.* Is time then an uncertain reality with which we nevertheless must live and die? I would willingly accept this perspective and follow the Buddhists, who believe that time is only an illusion. They add, however, that since we all live in a world that depends on this illusion, it is important that we perform each task in its proper time.

The time I will discuss here is neither the time of the philosophers nor that of the scientists; their theories are fascinating but have no practical application. The subject of this book is "perceived time": the time that allows humans to situate themselves throughout their existence, and the perception of this time, precisely because it varies enormously from one person to another, depending on who we are.

Let us equip ourselves then with a practical definition of time.

Time is our transformation

As a simple definition, let us say that time is that which measures a transformation. The transformation of a raw egg into a soft-boiled egg takes four minutes while the radioactive decay of carbon takes fourteen thousand years. You and I are between those two extremes. We tend to measure time by the changes in our own bodies. In the short term or in the long term? In the long term, as John Maynard Keynes noted, we are all dead.

We see our time against the background of death, our own or that of others. Nature provided our primitive ancestors with no other way of measuring the passage of time. They witnessed phenomena whose slow transformation was invisible to them (lakes, mountains, starry skies) or that seemed to recur in the same state (days and nights, the return of the seasons), giving rise to the idea, among Hindus, that time recurs eternally. Their belief in reincarnation allows them to transcend their own death and to take advantage of the infinite spiral of the centuries.

Many thousands of years before the invention of water clocks and hourglasses, the first instrument to measure time was probably . . . rheumatoid arthritis, that irritating sign of our fatal internal changes. The second was no doubt the mirror (still water or polished metal), a silent witness to our degradation. The passage of time is and always will be a personal experience or drama: *the hardest thing to bear as we get older is the feeling that we remain young inside.* The philosopher Simone Weil noted, "All the tragedies that we can imagine can be reduced to just one: the passage of time."

The most democratic of our resources

A SHARP pain in the kidneys, a resigned look in the mirror in the morning, seconds that escape from the quartz watch: these events give us no pleasure. But they force us to face the fact that time flies; and what are we going to do about it?

Our day-to-day vocabulary misleads us. The expressions "gaining time" or "losing time," we shall see, make no sense. *Each of us owns the whole of available time, which can be neither modified nor changed.* We have it in our power only to change our attitude toward it or to make good or bad use of it. But that is already something.

This fact leads to our first major conclusion: controlling time means controlling oneself.

If, philosophically, one can doubt the existence of time or view it merely as evidence of entropy, in an active life it is more practical to treat time as a resource that is essential, but one with very specific characteristics.

Like any resource, available time is to be *used*. It is the most democratically distributed resource. No matter whether you are powerful or wretched, enterprising or lazy, brilliant or stupid, everyone has, every day, the same amount of time to use. The difference, which may be great, comes from the way we use it.

We all have the same room

THE PARADOX of time is that few think they have enough of it, when in fact all of it is available to everyone.

Unlike other resources, time cannot be bought or sold, borrowed or stolen, saved up or put away, manufactured, multiplied, or modified. It can only be used. And, used or not, it disappears. *Of all resources, time is the most precious because it is the only one that is not renewable.*

But these are only concepts that we must try to translate into concrete images. The well-known relationship between space and time can help us because we are often more familiar with spatial metaphors than with temporal ones.

For a distance to be meaningful to us, we prefer to express it in terms of time (days of walking, hours of airplane flight, light-years) rather than in miles. It may be helpful to do the opposite and to consider time in terms of space.

Imagine that each of us, without exception, lives in a room exactly the same size. It is impossible to build another one or to enlarge it. We would differ only in the way in which we furnish the room.

Those who are insecure or eager to show off would buy a lot of furniture and one day would find they can no longer move in their overcrowded room. Some would not accumulate as many things but the arrangement would be disorderly and they would end up feeling disoriented and cramped. Some, by purchasing armoires, bureaus, and bookshelves, would make room for everything they need in the same space and would be able to move around with ease. Some, in order to make their room appear larger, would be content with a bed and almost nothing else.

It is easy to see that temperament and personality determine peoples' use of space and their way of life. Likewise with time.

Technology is a source of stress

MOST OF the inventions of the last century have allowed us to accomplish more in the same time. The car goes ten times as fast as the horse and the plane seven times as fast as the car. A microwave oven cooks chicken ten times as fast as the old-fashioned oven. The computer makes itself obsolete with every technological advance. The time necessary to accomplish most tasks has been considerably reduced.

Modern inventions also let us do several things simultaneously—to multitask, as we now say. Currently, the most common multitasking practice is to do something physical and something intellectual at the same time because performing two intellectual tasks at the same time leads to confusion or inattention. Many of us listen to the news while dressing, work while travelling, listen to music while typing letters—why not, now that it is possible to slip the CD directly into the disk drive—and, the most universal example, telephone while filing our nails or eating, cooking, walking or driving.

We have the feeling, in this way, of being speedy, clever, and powerful, since our ability to accomplish a task in a given time is incomparably greater than that of previous generations. But what was fun and surprising when we first got a cell phone soon becomes a constraint because those around us also have the same magical objects and use them frenetically.

Something that was developed to make our life easier quickly becomes an additional burden. Those who do not yet know how to use a computer feel themselves left behind by time and by the young. For them the struggle to make the most of their time leads them to question their ability to adapt.

Even those most adept at juggling the new technologies are often tired by the piles of written and oral messages, which, at ten o'clock at night, they have not yet answered.

Time remains impassive and inelastic and the most advanced computer chips can do nothing about it.

The nature of modern time

THE NATURE of time lived and perceived by human beings changes as they change. Let us look at the type of time which is ours because we live here (in a developed country) and now (at the dawn of the third millennium).

In contrast to the time of our ancestors, modern time is unified, rhythmic, and congested.

❖ Unified, for the whole planet is synchronized to the nearest thousandth of a second. The numbers assigned to the hours change, depending on the time zone, but the pulse of the time signal is now identical all over the globe as it is in space.

❖ Rhythmic, because we are bound by a network of social habits whose links are reckoned in time. We follow schedules for work, meetings, meals, business hours, the morning news or the evening movie, train departures, or infant feedings.

❖ Congested, for physical existence in this complex society has forced us to become busier and more productive than were our forebears. This significant increase in our output means that we must perform more activities in the fixed amount of time allotted to us.

The changes are quite recent. A hundred and fifty years ago, most people were peasants leading a life not unlike that of their ancestors centuries before. Of course, unlike their ancestors, they could know what time it was. They had no watches (too complicated and expensive), but the church bell sounded for morning, noon, and evening prayers.

Time then was very approximate, for each town, even each village, practiced its own. Tens of different times could exist within a small region. Sometimes, when politics became involved, the church bell signaled a different hour from the town hall clock.

In that life, human time was closer in nature to that of a cat, its rhythm set by the sun and consisting of periods of uninterrupted activities. We often think of those times with nostalgia even if, by our hyperactive standards, we feel they must have often been boring.

How stress was born

OUR RURAL ancestors experienced a new kind of stress when they had to report for outside work. When factories and mines transformed the sons and daughters of peasants into workers, they had to leave their homes each morning to reach the factory door at a specified time.

This was the first basic rupture in the continuity of natural time regulated by the seasons. The daily rhythm of life was set no longer by the light of the sun but by the opening and closing of the factory. In some plants it was even forbidden to know the time or wear a watch. The boss was the only master of time and decided the effective duration of the time imposed on his employees.

Later, the division of life caused by schedules accelerated because of the constant need to produce more. The stress of production was added to the stress of scheduling.

In the workplace the clock gave way to the chronometer. Since workers no longer produced their own food or clothes, they had to adapt to the hours of those who sold these things to them. When, much later, improved social conditions allowed them some leisure, they had to be on time for the beginning of a show or of a television program.

So it is that without wanting it, civilized people came to find themselves, like Gulliver among the Lilliputians, tied down by a multitude of subtle bonds, none individually strong enough to immobilize them but which together regulate their lives and deprive them of their freedom of movement.

Today stress has become one of the main causes of malaise. More than a quarter of women and 15 percent of men chronically complain of feeling stressed. But the main cause of stress is the result of a poor relationship with time. How can we not be feel stressed when we lack the time to accomplish everything that is expected of us: completing work that must be ready tomorrow, feeding the children and preparing to leave early for the airport, all on only four hours of sleep and after having answered an urgent phone call from a needy friend, and, at the same time, finished an essential task?

The best and most urgent reason for trying to improve how we use our time is to diminish the feeling of stress. It is an absolutely vital reason.

The march toward a unique time

DURING THE second half of the nineteenth century, the railroad brought about the universal synchronization of time.

Alone on his island, Robinson Crusoe had no need for a watch. But as soon as a community forms, its activities (meals, meetings, the education of children, religious services) must be regulated. Before industrialization an approximate schedule of activities sufficed. When one travels at the speed of the horse, one does not need to know what the time is in neighboring villages. But as soon as the railroad established a rapid, regional, national, and soon thereafter, international communication, people had to be able to predict the arrival and departure times of trains thousands of miles away. A single time system became essential.

For some years the train station clock did not necessarily tally with that of the steeple. But the eventual winner was predictable.

On both sides of the Atlantic, Europe and the United States synchronized their time before the beginning of the twentieth century. When the development of the telephone and radio communication put individuals in contact who had been separated by thousands of miles, precision became as essential as synchronization. Universal time is precise to the millionth of a second, thanks to quartz, which makes the watch today the most produced object in the world. Hence the French philosopher Michel Serre's statement: "From now on, everyone has a watch and no one has the time. Let us exchange one for the other: give away your watch and take your time."

It is too late, or perhaps too soon. One day perhaps, Serre's dream will become the ultimate luxury in our society of abundance.

Free time is shrinking

A FUNNY thing happened to Americans on their way to prosperity and better living. The richer they get, and the more they invent time-saving devices, like computers and frozen food, the more they work. It doesn't have to be so. In Western Europe, where people live equally well, free time increases constantly. The work week gets shorter—it is now around thirty-five to thirty-nine hours—with frequent vacations. In France, for instance, most workers have between six and eight weeks a year off. But not so in the United States.

A new study by the International Labor Organization found that the number of hours Americans work each year (1,966) has climbed skyward (the Japanese are next, at 1,889). On average, Americans work 350 hours (the equivalent of nine full workweeks) more per year than Europeans. One reason the American economy has seen its longest uninterrupted period of growth in its history is this: since 1980 the number of hours worked per person has increased 4 percent.

The percentage of Americans working very long schedules, of forty-nine hours per week or more, is on the rise—from 13 percent in 1976 to 19 percent in 1998, according to the U.S. Bureau of Statistics. People today work 160 hours more per year compared to thirty years ago. That's an extra month of work every year.

As for vacations, American employers seldom give more than ten paid days. This is not the American Dream, but the American paradox. Seen from a European point of view, it recalls the myth of Tantalus who, in hell, had an atrocious thirst and hunger, but who could not reach the delicious food in front of him. For Americans, it is as though the Protestant work ethic has enabled the creation of prosperity, but the nation's Puritan origins prevent its enjoyment.

Time has never been so scarce for Americans, nor stress so chronic. It may be good news to learn that something inexpensive can be done about it.

Can we take our time?

MODERN TECHNOLOGICAL life has strained our relationship to time. We are all caught in a painful contradiction, torn between our desire to do more and our profound need for leisure. We will see that only those who have learned to use it well can take advantage of time. But it is not only a question of temperament. We must create circumstances which favor a better relationship with time.

To disconnect from a hyperactive society, it is not enough to be on vacation. The breaks must be real, and we must have prepared for them. Laboratories that help us sever the ties of our daily lives already exist on every continent; for example, there are Club Meds and other resorts inspired by their success. These laboratories satisfy three essential conditions:

1. They create a small community with no relation to the outside world: no television, no telephone, and faxes that reach you with difficulty.
2. Everything is provided in abundance.
3. The individual does not have to do anything, not even get out of bed.

This setting, however, does not preclude the wearing of a watch since even if meals are announced noisily, the activities are scheduled. Only the real *far niente* ("do nothing" in Italian) can free us for a few days from our servitude to time. Who is fully capable of such freedom?

In order to break our daily rhythm for a week or two every year, we watch-wearers are obliged, the rest of the time, to a rigorous personal productivity based on precise timing.

We choose the moment

THE MORE technology progresses, the more we are able to bottle time in order to use it as we choose. The idea of disconnecting time from an action and its consequences is not entirely new, but it has achieved a strikingly wide scope.

For you to listen to a sonata composed by Mozart two centuries ago, the composer had to first fix the melody in a score using a code, that of musical notation. Then, one day, long ago, an orchestra assembled to make the same music from these notes that a recording enables us to hear today. So we benefit from a double jump in time: from the moment of Mozart's creation and from that of the orchestra's performance.

Writing is the most widespread code that has allowed ideas and words to outlive their author. Every library looks like the heavens that simultaneously bombard our retina with the light emitted by a star "only" a century ago and that emitted by a galaxy millions of years ago. In the same way, from between the covers of books come a message from Plato written some twenty-five hundred years ago, another from Pascal written three hundred years ago, and a third from Camus written "only" forty years ago. It is writing, not printing, that enables people to separate the genesis of an idea from its perception. Gutenberg introduced an effect not in time but in space, by making writing universally, and eventually cheaply, available.

Today the ability to separate production from use has spread because of the proliferation of machines. The freezer allows us to consume a dish cooked a week ago, the VCR to see Thursday's program on Sunday, and the Internet to hear a radio program broadcast years ago. And then there are all the messages, spoken or written, that quietly await our attention. *If we cannot change time, we can play with the order and with the moment.*

A university professor who did not have time to give his class asked an assistant to play his taped lectures to his students. Two weeks later, he unexpectedly visited his class and found only, on a table, his tape recorder surrounded by those of his students.

If we know how to make use of them, these different ways of manipulating time can give us unimaginable freedom to organize our life to fit our own rhythm.

Time is money

THE EXPRESSION that most irritates European humanists is the famous American saying that "time is money."

How can the hours of our lives be reduced to such a simple financial valuation? Of course such an equation is laughable, but let us admit that the hourly wage is a permanent reference point in social debates. And the rate of interest (that is, the cost of money over a certain period) is watched with equal fascination by families seeking housing and by the highest financial authorities. Whether we like it or not, time, whether it concerns individuals or services, has a price.

Any price has psychological consequences. Imagine that a brilliant lawyer or consultant to multinationals notices, at ten o'clock, that she has a run in her pantyhose. She must change quickly before meeting a client for lunch, but there are no stores nearby. To go out and buy a new pair will take an hour. She bills her clients at the rate of $500 an hour. She is dismayed to realize that the pair of pantyhose will end up costing her $520. The price seems unreasonable to her, but can she remain with a run in her stockings?

Every moment has a price, even if it is not necessarily a monetary one. Is an hour of reading "worth" as much as an hour of play with your eight-year-old? Is an extra hour of work worth an hour of sleep? In the words of the humorist Tristan Bernard, "There are people who make you lose a whole day in five minutes."

It is not surprising that time has a *value*, in all the meanings of that word, since it is our most precious resource. Often, money may be viewed as deferred time. Your bank account is the result of the work that allows you to defer your enjoyment. Your retirement has been financed by an assessment paid over many years of work.

The relationship between money and the time available to us is necessarily ambiguous. On the one hand, money allows us to make our wishes come true by paying with our capital of time; on the other hand, it allows us to control our time by purchasing the timesaving machines that, more and more, are a necessary part of our furnishings.

When we become aware of this ambiguity, we realize that money is only a neutral tool to be used well or badly. Time remains the central problem, because it regulates and measures our life.

Jet lag

WHAT DO business people who fly long distances talk about in airport lounges? They talk about jet lag. Everyone has a trick to overcome the insomnia followed by a down period that is the symptom of jet lag. Melatonin currently is considered the most effective remedy.

Very young managers do not even know that the notion of jet lag is only about fifty years old. To be aware of it, international air travel, just like the telephone, had to become part of our daily life.

When Atlantic crossings took five days on boats, travelers moved their watches ahead or back one hour every evening. Thus they were already adapted to the local time on arrival.

Today some people are able to board the first machine to go backward in time: the Concorde, a financial disaster but a fabulous symbol of modern time. You can leave Paris at eleven o'clock and land at Kennedy at eight o'clock, thus arriving three hours before you left. The fact that these 180 minutes "gained" cost each passenger six months of the French minimum monthly wage does not prevent them from feeling that they have gained a symbolic, if ephemeral, victory over time.

This triumph is of course only symbolic since the passengers on the Concorde have not pushed back the hands of the only real clock, their biological clock. But, even though they have not been rejuvenated by three hours, they have treated themselves to the most luxurious method of mastering time.

In order to maximize the Concorde effect, some executives leave their office in Paris after an hour of work on Monday morning. They land in New York at the start of the American work day and make full use of it before returning to Paris on a regular plane on which they have reserved three coach seats (which cost as much as the supersonic flight) so they can stretch out and sleep for six hours. On Tuesday morning they resume their work in Paris free of fatigue and jet lag.

But let us not kid ourselves. Working Monday on Park Avenue and Tuesday on the Champs-Elysées, they have abolished not time but distance, through an optimal use of time.

The ecology of time

THE RACE after time is a modern sickness. How many times have we heard the praise of a past in which everything seemed more peaceful and the pace was slower? How many documentaries have we seen about societies in which the rhythm of life seems closer to that of nature? Marcel Proust's *Remembrance of Things Past*, the first great novel of the twentieth century, continues to express, a hundred years after it was first published, a nostalgia for another way of life—a slower way.

The preoccupation with time is at least a sign of progress, since it forces us to consider and study the very fabric of our existence.

When we become aware that modern time is profoundly different from that experienced by our ancestors, we understand that progress has treated time the way it has treated nature—it has used them both unreflectively, as if there were a limitless supply.

Water, air, greenery, and time were greedily attacked for a hundred and fifty years before we realized that they were both vital and perishable.

In the same way that we have become aware of our natural surroundings (the battle is not yet won), we must become aware of our personal time. But our awareness of time is different in a fundamental way: nature exists outside of us, but personal time exists only for us and only as long as we live. We can tell ourselves that we are not (or only somewhat) responsible for global warming and industrial pollution. But no one will ever be more responsible than we for the quality of our time.

You Run After Time

How time regained is taken from us · Productivity makes us schiz-
ophrenic · We have less time to choose · We buy without thinking
· Our bulimia of consumption · An hour a day for our pleasures ·
We live in multiple times · Our meetings with the phagocytes ·
The king of time-wasters is in my pocket · Seven minutes of quiet
· Waiting is intolerable · How to make bad decisions · The basic
matter of love · Stressed rather than obese

How time regained is taken from us

IN THE early 1950s, less than one percent of households
in Western Europe had a television set. Today there is at
least one in every home and the average person watches it
three hours a day, more than 10 percent of the inextensible
number of hours in a day.

Now a new screen, the Internet, has begun its galloping
invasion. In the United States, where over a third of the
population is connected from home, people spend on the
average more than an hour a day surfing the Internet. The

time they devote to various media is now distributed in this way: 30 percent is spent on the computer, 30 percent in front of a TV set, 25 percent is devoted to radio and only 16 percent to print media.

In France only three million regularly visit the Web, but these numbers will triple in the first few years of the new century. This "media time" will be taken from the time spent on other activities. It will *take time from* sleeping or playing or reading or puttering, or it will *take place at the same time* as meals or family gatherings, in other words *at the expense of* conversation or feeling or concentration or internal peace.

Now, although we must work in order to eat, and sleep in order to rest, we are not compelled to watch television or to sit in front of a computer monitor. Try to explain this to someone who devotes several evenings a week to these activities and who at the same time complains (it is common) of no longer having enough time to read or to sleep. Will he or she give them up? The bets are open.

We can accept the growing importance of interactivity as an irreversible characteristic of modernity. It is not possible to give it up in the name of a lost serenity any more than it is possible to give up the telephone or the automobile, both of which make us lose as well as gain time. However, we must come to terms with the fact that *these tools that free us from time also devour the surplus they create.*

It is up to us to choose consciously what we are prepared to sacrifice. Puttering around? Maybe. Concentration and inner peace? Let us think about these.

Productivity makes us schizophrenic

THE PRESENT congestion of our personal time is due in part to our growing demands . . . or is it because we are weak? But let us not lay a guilt trip on ourselves. It also has its roots in three aspects of our economic system: productivity, dispersal, and consumption.

Productivity is at once the miracle and the curse of our advanced society. Since it allows fewer and fewer people to produce more and more, it constantly lowers the price of industrial and agricultural products, and it lays off those who are no longer needed. Those who are kept on, on the other hand, have more and more work. In the mid-nineteenth century half of the population in Europe or in the U.S. was employed in the agricultural sector. Today there are less than 2 percent farmers left, but they feed twice as many people.

Two recent trends have pushed productivity to new highs: globalization, which forces each business to compete with those that are most efficient, no matter where they are located, and social progress which reduces working time and increases vacations. And so productivity gives us free time and lowers prices. But while we are at work, which we are most of the time, it forces us to be more and more efficient and therefore more and more tense.

Our attitude toward time is therefore double-edged. At work there is no question of relaxing. We must employ all the known formulas and the possible technologies to make the best use of our time. On the other hand, during our personal time, that which belongs to us alone and to our loved ones, we must forget productivity and think about well-being and replenishment. This internal flexing is a little schizophrenic, isn't it? A little, in fact, but let us use it to develop and expend our ability to use time.

We have less time to choose

IN ORDER to function, our society breaks up our time by dispersing our life. This dispersal is added to the tensions of our professional life and is chiefly expressed in commuting time. Not only is the workplace dissociated from where we live, but the distance between home and job is increasing. Large supermarkets are rarely located near our homes, our children do not necessarily attend a neighborhood school, our parents live far away, our medical specialists practice in distant hospitals and our leisure hours are spent far from home and work. We end up wasting a great many of the hours which social progress and time-saving appliances have given us.

And let us not forget our sacred duty to consume. Most of us seem to have forgotten to take into account the fact that consuming takes time. The increase in our purchasing power has allowed each of us to increase his and her consumption, but the time available for this consumption has not increased correspondingly.

Faced with a major purchase such as a car, a stereo or a TV, a home or apartment, we think of ascertaining the price and the method of financing. But who thinks about the budget of time connected to it: choice + upkeep + enjoyment=?

The increasing technical complexity and profusion of the objects available to us should lead the rational consumer (who we claim to be) to compare the price and quality of every purchase. Do you really do this when you buy your VCR or your washing machine?

For lack of time, the more lavish and complicated the products, the poorer the quality of our buying decisions. With our tacit consent, our choices are often largely determined by advertising. We ignorant consumers assuage our guilt by accepting the arguments proposed to us by clever advertisements.

If we are to believe Bill Gates and everyone in Silicon Valley, in the future the Internet will change everything. We will search, compare, and buy without moving from home. Won't that be the ideal way of settling all those annoying problems of control? There are now Web sites on which you can hear the noise the refrigerator door makes when you close it—a feature important to some buyers. It would not surprise me if this miraculous tool eats up as much of our time as it saves us, if not more.

We buy without thinking

LEISURE TIME or upkeep time? How many hours does a sailboat owner spend sand-papering it or rigging it compared with the time he is out sailing it? How much time does the owner of a pool spend cleaning it rather than swimming in it? How many days does it take to keep up your country house compared to the time you enjoy in it? Unless your way of enjoying your garden is in fact to garden?

Leisure time: rise up, books purchased but never read, CDs heard only once, clothes hardly worn, television programs recorded and never watched! Our attics are full of roller skates, rowing machines, bicycles bought on an impulse, with no thought of the number of hours it would take to actually use them. If the cost of our second homes were divided by the number of days we actually spend there (without overlooking the interest on the money tied up in frozen assets) we might realize that often we could rent a sumptuous vacation house for the same time and still have money to put aside.

And for those people who feel they do take advantage of their second home, do they ever dream of the trips they did not take because they had to justify the second home?

From the point of view of the use of time, consumption is our century's great neurosis, at least if we use the least clinical definition of neurosis as that which makes an intelligent person do something stupid.

The genius of Henry Ford (who started out as a watchmaker) lay in paying his workers enough to allow them to buy the cars they manufactured. Haven't we adopted this principle at our expense when we use what we earn to purchase the objects and services we manufacture, without being sure that we are living better?

Our bulimia of consumption

OUR BULIMIA of consumption not only eats our time but eats itself as well. Our skills at consuming, however, remain primitive. We think much more about the use of our money which is renewable, than about our time, which is irreplaceable.

We switch on a sophisticated and expensive sound system to create a background noise to which we listen with only half our attention. We have the capability of listening to an opera at home, quietly and without doing anything else, in conditions resembling those of a real concert hall. How often have we done that?

We have neither the time to do our shopping calmly nor to cook delicious dishes. At the last minute we order expensive pizzas or Chinese food, which are not at all healthful. We gain time but we lose the pleasure of living.

We set off for the ends of the earth after having tracked down the cheapest charter flight, rather than become steeped in the culture and history of the country to which we are flying. Once there, we look at faces and landscape through the lens of our Nikon. And we are left with little time to savor their difference, and even less time to look at the pictures or videos we spent our time taking.

We get together with our friends at noisy and crowded receptions or at dinner parties where the conversation is leveled to the least common denominator. But we rarely take the time to meet our friends one on one or two by two.

We have thus the feeling of seeing them often, without really knowing who they are, nor what is happening in their lives and what they think.

We are encouraged to critique the "consumer society." But is this for ethical reasons or is it because the consumer society has not brought us the satisfactions we expect? In fact, the chief cause of our disappointment is our bulimia, which leads us to telescope or pile up our sources of pleasure.

An hour a day for our pleasures

WE DEVOTE bits of time to a multitude of pleasures instead of enjoying at leisure the rare pleasures that truly suit us. That is because, in spite of our "available" time, the hours that are wholly ours are rare.

Let us do some arithmetic. It takes some 40 percent of our day to satisfy our biological needs: sleeping (7 hours), eating (2 hours), dressing and personal care (1 hour)—ten hours in all. In order to pay for these needs (and for our lodging, medical care, heating, and that which makes life pleasant), we must work (8 hours + 1 hour of commuting)—9 hours. So the time devoted to needs is 19 hours (or 20 to 21 if you add a minimum of housework and shopping). That leaves us four hours for the ordinary pleasures (family life, entertainment, learning, sports, etc.). But let us not forget the three hours spent in front of the TV screen. Do we then have only one hour left of real available time?

That is not much, is it? But let us remember where we started. At the beginning of the industrial era, people worked twelve hours and slept at least one hour more than we do in order to recuperate. Their time for necessities took almost the entire twenty-four hour day. No time was left for pleasure other than at a large village or family gathering three or four times a year, which was just as well since no one had a dime to spare. In comparison to them we have some free time and an income that allows us to pay for more than our basic needs.

The trouble is that, although we can satisfy our measurable needs—we need only three meals a day—our desires are limitless, especially since our culture, through advertising and the bombardment of information, sharpens our desires by constantly inventing new ones.

We are more refined, more imaginative, more prosperous; how can we not be more demanding? But our wants always increase faster than the time available to satisfy them. And that is the basic reason why we have the feeling that we do not have enough time.

We live in multiple times

UNTIL THE seventeenth century, from the time of the Greeks on, playwrights obeyed the law of three unities: unity of space, of action, and of time. The lives of the great majority of the population followed these same laws. The brief life of the villagers was defined by their occupation, station in life, and the need to bring up a single family.

Until the middle of the nineteenth century, the individual lived in well-defined pigeonholes: one spouse, one employer, often only one home. In these three domains, the very idea of mobility was looked at askance. Life went on in these well-defined molds, without surprise. Those who did not fit these molds were considered to be adventurers; they were secretly envied, perhaps, but often disapproved of.

After World War II, however, our time became seriously fractured. Since then, for most of us, displacements—in the neighborhood, the city, or even the country—cut our lifetimes into geographical slices; changes of jobs into professional slices, successive partners into emotional slices, and stepfamilies into familial slices. And since the combination of these four displacements is not necessarily simultaneous, it provides many excuses for muddled memories.

We have substituted a long life with multiple and mixed times for a short life with few times.

Some Buddhists admit that their theory of successive lives does not necessarily imply reincarnation. They note that each of us goes through several lives, perhaps even from one day to the next. When we look back at who we were ten or twenty years ago, doesn't that person seem to be someone other than the one we have become?

We are faced with a philosophical question. If all the elements of our life change one after the other, what remains constant in us? A weave of memories which fade with time?

Our meetings with the phagocytes

OUR TIME is fractured to the point of atomization by the constant collision with the time of others. We come into contact with more and more people who have easy access to us through various means of communication, and the pressure on us to respond is greater.

Cast a pebble into a calm pond and perfect concentric circles expand lazily until calm returns to the surface. But let a hailstorm rage, peppering the surface, and thousands of circles intersect and form a chaotic infinitude of wavelets. The water becomes turbid. That is how the time of others scrambles up our own.

In the not so distant past, rural time was like a calm pond: few meetings, few interactions. Towns stayed small, like the work units that they harbored.

Today, even if it happens that we are alone in a crowd, we feel hemmed in. In the megalopolises we inhabit, the businesses we work in, we come into daily contact with hundreds of our peers.

It is estimated that each one of us knows an average of some thousand people, if not more. Even if only a hundred of them have regular access to us (family, colleagues, friends, service people, clients, neighbors, relatives, etc.) these are just so many opportunities for successive and uncontrollable interruptions. *Each person who comes into contact with us is, consciously or unconsciously, preying on our precious and irreplaceable time.* And likewise we prey on his or hers.

At the heart of this realization is an ambiguity: few of us would wish to live solitary lives. To mix our time with that of others: isn't that precisely what gives us life? Don't we miss it when the stream of relationships dries out?

But, as in nearly every area, when a pleasure is abused it turns first into an annoyance and then into a nightmare.

Don't we all feel that beyond a certain number of children, coworkers, family and friends, the problem of time does not even come up since it is entirely consumed by them?

The king of time-wasters is in my pocket

IN THE era of the handwritten letter delivered on foot or on horseback, how many messages were sent and received each day? How many visits could one make by horse or carriage, how many voyages by boat? Famous lovers might exchange no more than one or two letters a day.

All of a sudden, a little more than a hundred years ago, the telephone appeared. In the early days, sensible people took offense. The French actor Lucien Guitry (born in 1860) said disdainfully: "Someone rings you and like a servant you respond?"

During the first fifty years, people considered it a privilege to have a telephone. Those who had one saved a great deal of time and felt linked to the entire planet. Not until the last quarter of the twentieth century did each French family have a telephone. And then everything went very fast. Most of those who had adolescents living at home installed a second line. In some cities, such as Washington, D.C., there are more telephones than inhabitants.

At the same time diabolical technologies have been perfected. Answering machines make sure that no call will fail to get through to us. "Call-forwarding" devices allow pests to hound us at our friends' or in another office. "Call-waiting" mechanisms produce delightful interruptions in a conversation by a caller who is not aware that she or he is breaking in. The end of the twentieth century witnessed the appearance of the Terminator of communication: the cellular phone.

Thanks to this king of time-destroyers, anyone can interrupt a crucial negotiation, a family meal, a moment of creative reflection or worship, your sleep, your shower, your moments of tenderness or of private enjoyment at the theater or concert hall . . . That is, if you wish so, because luckily voice mail was developed almost simultaneously. *Many have learned to use these fashionable tools . . . in order to make themselves inaccessible.*

In the growing battle for control of our time, the mobile telephone has become for all of us what the Kalashnikov is for a terrorist: an indispensable weapon of attack or of defense.

Seven minutes of quiet

EVERYTHING CONSPIRES to transform our time into chopped meat: the multiplication of our tasks, the continually increasing number of people with whom we come in contact and the continual invention of new means of communication which maintain these contacts.

It is not surprising that many people say: "When I have to concentrate on my work, I stay home." That is when the conditions at work allow it. As for mothers, they can work at home only until the children come home from school, for after that, there is no question of thinking.

Our little darlings have quickly learned how to interrupt

their parents' lives even from a distance. Ever since mommy and daddy acquired a cell phone, the calls about this and that come fast after school: "How are you, mom? And how is daddy? What time are you coming home? What's for dinner?" Mommy complains that she's in a meeting but she only buys a half hour of peace, because the calls soon resume. And of course, as soon as they are seven years old, they start to ask for their own cell phone. How long can the parents resist?

In the meantime, at work, any manager, according to studies, is interrupted on the average every seven minutes by a phone call, an unexpected visit, or a question from a colleague. One can imagine the inefficiency, the stress, and most of all, the poor quality of thinking which results of it.

Interruption is the rule, no matter the situation, to the point where one must admire our ability to adapt to this neurotic way of life. Because things do get done, more or less.

But this leads to a troubling question: what if the complaint that we are overworked provides us with a good excuse for not thinking? And what if we have created this swarming society because it corresponds to a profound human need for frenetic diversion that keeps us from noticing the passage of time?

Waiting is intolerable

TIME TORMENTS us. We luxuriate in it so as to forget it, we speed it up while hoping to outdistance it. Even if this irrational thinking is unconscious, it produces troubling changes in the modern individual, such as the fear of waiting and the inability to concentrate.

As early as 1907, the French philosopher Henri Bergson noted: "If I want a cup of coffee, I have to wait for the sugar to melt." He would surely be relieved to discover that, thanks to modern technology, the sugar cube today melts four times as fast, but still not immediately. Herman Kahn, the futurologist, told me that when as a child when he asked for a bicycle, his parents replied: "A bicycle is expensive. Maybe next year . . . ." He noted that for his grandson, "next year" is the same as "never."

The most sophisticated means of communication is now the television spot, because everything must be said in thirty seconds or less. Extremely complicated and often spectacular, many cost several hundred thousands of dollars to produce, even more in some cases like those aired during the Super Bowl.

On the computer, a response time of five seconds can seem endless. We trade up for a faster machine with more RAM and megs of memory. Educational researchers have also found that a teacher waits less than one second before getting convinced that his pupil is not going to answer a question.

Our chronic impatience has, in addition, the most pernicious effect on our ability to concentrate. In our daily life, we take into account only the time to do, to act; the time to reflect—before and after—has vanished into thin air. We make most of our decisions on the spot, by intuition, and we find that normal. Businesses pay consultants a great deal to think about problems, which their own employees understand better, but about which they don't have the time to think soberly.

Sprinters of action, we lack the wind for the long-distance race of reflection.

How to make bad decisions

ALMOST WITHOUT our knowledge, the amount of information available to us has literally exploded. We have not yet become aware of the consequences of this eruption.

When the current crop of adults were children, there still was widespread agreement about who was cultivated or culturally literate. Those who pursued their studies could run through the canonical literature. Our cultural and artistic references could be shared with our cohort. And, for most people, the existence of three television channels, meant that everyone received more or less the same information and could comment on the same entertainment.

All of this has become atomized. Three times as many books and magazines are now published. The number of available television channels has increased to the point that we cannot even run through all of them. More than a thousand Web sites are now being created each day. The electronic media have certainly created the global village predicted by Marshall McLuhan, but our ability to absorb the images, the information, and the ideas has not changed. So except for the narrow domain of our own competence, we know even less about nearly everything. Our own knowledge is full of holes that become larger much more quickly than do the solid islands.

The only thing that cannot grow in the modern world is the length of our days. We have more days of life, since our life expectancy is longer. But the length of each day remains the same. Each of us can feel the consequences.

In business as in politics, decision-makers rarely depend on first-hand data they themselves have gathered and analyzed. They must accept the conclusions or the summaries of experts (market studies, commission reports) which often do not share the same values and standards. And so choices with national ramifications and serious financial consequences are made on the basis of incomplete information. These choices are then followed by reversals, often at the highest national level.

Because of our stressed approach to time we do nothing thoroughly in order to do more. Impatient and therefore superficial, we avoid asking profound questions. And when we must answer our own legitimate preoccupations concerning our motives or our way of life, we call that an existential crisis.

Our obsession with the "how" and the "how much" keeps us at a comfortable distance from the "why."

The basic matter of love

TIME-CHOPPING spares nothing and most of all not love. Love is not stated; it is proven by time spent. Working mothers count the hours spent with their children, either to reassure themselves or to feel guilty. Friendships also require an investment of time. As for romantic love, it is a plant that must be watered with hours and days of intimacy.

Alas, romantic love also wastes away for lack of nourishment. Courting means using outmoded circumlocutions—and patience. Maintaining a relationship demands an investment of time whose productivity is no longer assured.

We have come to believe that love happens right away or not at all.

Today lovers spend more time on the telephone than in bed.

If conjugal fidelity is on the rise, it may be more as a result of the pace of life than of changing morality.

Even when people love each other and spend time together, the quality of their sexual life depends on the time they can devote to it. As soon as a troubling element appears such as a business trip or a big project, urgent housework, and more than anything, worry about children and family, sexuality declines. Most couples who get along well yearn for the same thing: time to be alone, elsewhere, without interruptions.

Women complain that it is hard to be a working mother. The times are incompatible. And if you ask them about their love life, they sigh: "something has to give." They find the choices more and more difficult.

There is no art of love without an art of time.

Stressed rather than obese

IN THE industrialized countries, when a perpetual scarcity of food was succeeded by relative abundance, people did not resist. They began gorging themselves and the richer they became the fatter they grew. Many died as a result. A few generations later, they looked at themselves and found their bodies ugly and uncomfortable. So reaction set in in the form of articles, books, and programs, until excess weight became a global concern.

We have made progress because the new values of health and beauty are dominant. Our bodies no longer resemble those of our grandparents. We all watch what we eat. Unfortunately, perhaps because the consequences of the poor use of time are less visible than the consequences than a poor diet, the problem has not yet become a national priority. Nevertheless, it can make us as sick as does overeating. Ulcers, heart attacks, or cancers grow in the wake of stress, which is to time what obesity is to food. But in a sense this situation is much more serious because many more people suffer from stress than from obesity. And while we may meet or know fat people who are happy, those without enough time rarely experience any joy in life.

There is no diet of time. However, we have the greatest need of one because our well-being, our happiness, and probably the very meaning of our life are threatened.

Let us begin by trying to understand how, personally, we reached this point.

Up to this point we measured the extent to which mod-

43

ern life abuses the ancestral natural time by which humanity believed itself firmly defined. Destabilized and giddy and sometimes out of breath we ask ourselves before such upheavals if we can ever regain our lost equilibrium.

For each of us, the process of reconquering time involves awareness of our condition and an achievement of mastery, a genuine reeducation.

THE TEMPO OF YOUR TIME

*The end of the vacation • Nature's time, a comfortable illusion •
Social time hems us in • Experienced time, not philosophical time
• It is time to react • The first constraints • Those who make us
wait • The wondrous memory of the present • In search of the
temporal horizon • We are paid to see far into the future •
The time you need for each thing • To each, his or her own time*

The end of the vacation

WHETHER YOU have a week or a month, at a certain point
in your vacation, time begins to accelerate. At first, the end
seems so far off that you can afford not to think about it. We
feel we have a wealth of leisure, as when our bank account
is full at the beginning of the month and we worry less about
spending. These are our crumbs of eternity.

We can still fantasize that we will be able to read three
books, take a two-day trip, take up windsurfing, play chess

with the children, and spend long evenings talking with friends. The time of our dreams is expandable.

This feeling that time's course has slackened is in fact the chief benefit we expect from a vacation: to break the rhythm. Isn't even the word "vacation" a synonym for availability?

And then one day we return to reality. Once again we see the horizon approaching. The remaining days seem to shorten and can no longer hold everything we had planned to do. We are still on vacation but we must now begin to choose: the book that we won't read, the trip we won't make. Although we are not yet back in harness, we feel the constraint of time.

When does this tilt occur? For those prone to anxiety, it happens after two days; for the lighthearted, on the last evening. For me, it takes place at midpoint, whatever that may be.

It is the same, of course, with life.

At the age of ten, a year seems a century; at forty, a brief interlude. The subjective duration of time varies during the course of our life.

Up to now, we have described a solid, unyielding, and electronic time, and suddenly we realize it can be distorted like a marshmallow. Are we still talking about the same time?

Of course not, because we live according to a triple beat: nature's time, society's time, and experienced time— our own time.

Nature's time, a comfortable illusion

NATURE'S TIME, first of all, is cosmic time, that of the fifteen billion or so years since the Big Bang. We are still unsure whether the universe will go on expanding indefinitely or whether it will contract in a scientific pulsation until a new explosion creates other worlds. It is so much beyond us or seems so repetitive that it has only a metaphysical influence on our earthly passage. This time could not care less if human beings existed on the planet or not.

Oddly, this fundamental datum is a recent discovery. Until the end of the nineteenth century the history of the earth was measured in thousands rather than in billions of years. Basing himself on the Bible, Western man naively sought to be the measure of the universe that he believed was created for him. And then everything accelerated, to the detriment of our human and terrestrial ego. Astrophysicists informed us that the universe came from far away, that our Earth was young and—and this is a depressing detail—that it will certainly be absorbed in the final fireworks produced by the star Sun, before another five billion years.

The most important consequences of these facts for the individual are philosophical: the human being who thought he was at the center of the universe is relegated to the rank of a phenomenon which, while interesting, is ephemeral and whose reason for being becomes even more mysterious.

The perception of nature's time is completely beyond us. Even if we (that is, scientists) are capable of calculating it, we cannot conceive it. The time of the universe gives us a concrete taste of the infinite and the eternal while maintaining the mystery of existence. More modestly, that time is the one of our suburban solar system, with day and night, hot and cold, green and white. Nature's time is also that of the seasons and of the weather, a time to which we are infinitely sensitive. Our mood and our feelings change depending on whether the day is sunny or gray. But because nature's time is repetitive, it contributes to the illusion of an annual beginning and hides from us the inevitable flight of the time of our life.

Social time hems us in

SOCIAL TIME, modern time, on the other hand, holds us in its close embrace. Arising from the proliferation and acceleration of interpersonal relations, it remains a convention. On a desert island, we would immediately cast off these oppressive social garments. But there are no more desert islands and, if there were, we probably would not go there willingly.

Social time is made up of two very different components: the first is imposed on us—the years, days, and hours—and we construct the second—meetings and routines.

From birth to death, the temporal frame of our life may appear predictable and fixed, like a grid that will be filled. And that is what happens, whether we want it or not, from the day when we first enter primary school.

Our school years, which have their own rhythm, are followed by the years of work, and then by the retirement years. On this basic framework we impose our own way of organizing our days according to our role in society and our tastes.

In this manner grows the web of which we are at the same time the spider and the fly.

In the early years of our social autonomy, after we have completed our studies, we think we can choose the way we use our time. It is the sign of our freedom, until we realize that it is essentially predetermined by our profession, our age, our family situation, and our income. To "have free time" seems more and more an illusion, to the point when we feel, in moments of depression, that we are bullied by everyone.

To keep from being alienated or overwhelmed by it, we clearly have a stake in knowing the rules and management of social time. For skilled players, the gain may be substantial. It adds up to freedom.

Experienced time, not philosophical time

EXPERIENCED TIME, on a daily basis, is intimately mingled with social time, but we must not confuse the two. Made up of perceptions, feelings, and biology, experienced time is throughout our life the most "real" of the three times. *Our consciousness does not perceive time, which, we have seen, is often an abstract concept, but duration, whose consistency varies depending on our state of being.* This perceived duration is the very stuff of our existence and cannot be defined by the codes of social time. Terms associated with it, such as "long" or "short," "calm" or "crazy," "exciting" or "sinister" describe it much better than "minute" or "week" or "trimester." This time is expressed qualitatively, whereas social time is mostly quantified.

André Comte-Sponville, a philosopher, described it with his characteristic clarity: "The time of consciousness is different from the time of clocks, in the same way as the philosophers say subjective time differs from objective time. . . . This knowledge, which is not really knowledge and which precedes all knowledge, is what we call consciousness. We must remind ourselves that it is thoroughly temporary. And that it is not homogeneous in the way of the world or of clocks. Otherwise, would we even need clocks? . . . Our time—experienced time, the time of conscience and heart—is multiple, heterogeneous, uneven. It is as if it refracted and multiplied in us depending on whether it did or did not come in contact with our desires, on whether it accompanied them or resisted them, depending on whether it used them or exalted them. . . . There is no point in dwelling on it. Philosophy is not for describing, analyzing or endlessly commenting the truths of our common consciousness, which are sufficient unto themselves and which are almost always worth more than all the talk surrounding them."

I will devote the rest of this book to perceived time, or the time of our consciousness. If this examination teaches us nothing about the nature of time, it will shed a useful light on the way we live now and therefore on our unique and concrete life.

It is time to react

IN EXPERIENCED time, an hour or a year do not have the same subjective duration for people at different stages of life or in different emotional circumstances. This perceived time is also that of affectivity, of creation, of pleasure, of knowledge, and of thinking. It is as fragile as it is essential, for it is interlaced with social time which, like a clinging vine, may end up choking the host plant.

It is experienced time that, to different degrees, we feel is lacking; to some it is merely a memory which often goes back to adolescence, before the taking on of responsibility.

Why, for example, does time seem to shrink as we grow older? In general, after thirty, we feel trapped. External pressures make increasing demands on us. Our weightiest professional responsibilities coincide with the most exacting family obligations. Our "room" fills quickly up, to the point where we no longer have any space in which to maneuver.

It is usually during these years that we face our mortality for the first time. Just as at a certain point during our vacation the horizon of the holiday's end suddenly becomes visible, we lose the illusion of immortality that is so widespread among the young.

The realization that our stock of time is limited and nonrenewable and that each day irrevocably amputates it suddenly gives to each day a special quality.

With the approach of maturity, the hours become subjectively rarer and more precious. This is the critical period in our relation to time. At the age of eighty-five, Pa Kin, the greatest contemporary Chinese writer, had just been decorated by François Mitterand and was invited to come to France. "To do what? To meet whom? To learn why that is interesting?" he asked. "You realize," he added, as if to apologize for these questions, "I feel as if I have only seven dollars left in my pocket, and I don't want to use them to buy peanuts."

Often, then, we feel the time has come to react, to go from spending time carelessly to guarding it jealously.

It happens in the present.

When it becomes clear to us that we must not waste our days, few of us possess a suitable approach or method for utilizing them.

"Time," writes Comte-Sponville, "is first the succession of the past, the present, and the future. But the past no longer exists nor does the future since it doesn't exist yet."

In practice, only the present counts, for that is where we spend our life and it is unimaginable that we could be elsewhere.

The present of our past consists of our memories. We can be there in our thoughts but we cannot live there. The present of our future consists of our projects. Their execution absorbs us, but in the present, and until they also become present. Putting the past, present, and future on the same plane completely falsifies our perception of time that is made up only of the present. Nevertheless, this is a common mistake. It may be understandable but it is nevertheless a dangerous one if you want to live your life in the best possible way.

Pediatricians have suggested that some twelve years go by before a child fully assimilates the mechanics of time.

Usually she learns to tell time before the age of eight. Then she organizes in her mind the articulation of days, months, and years. But these are only codes, as different from inwardly perceived time as the reading of numbers on dollar bills is from having a sense of the value of money.

The important thing is to understand how our perception of time is formed and how it evolves. Too few studies have been done. We note only that, as with affectivity and with moral values, the example of our parents marks us in the way we treat the hours.

The first constraints

ARE WE punctual because our parents insisted that we respect the clock, or do we refuse to follow a timetable because we were forced to eat at six on the dot night after night? In either case, it is useful to look back. Recalling the way our parents viewed appointments, delays, and family projects will help explain what remains with us or against which we have reacted.

The constraints of time, at least those imposed from the outside, are learned in school, the family, and . . . from television.

Obligatory schedules (including punishments or excuses), hour-long classes, changes in programs because of the days of the week, waiting for weekends and vacations, all that we learn in school.

We inherit from our family whether we wake up by ourselves or with the help of others, whether we schedule mealtimes or not, whether or not we leave the house at the last minute. Add to that, of course, plans for the afternoon or evening for our favorite and/or permitted television programs.

This amalgam constitutes a quite substantial restraint. If you throw in some sports practice on Wednesday afternoon and one or two rehearsals, our stressed children will have every reason to view any rigid schedule with horror. And those who conform willingly to such a tempo should even cause us some concern.

Just as a premature interest in theology yields future agnostics, a tyrannic schedule imposed on ten-year-olds runs the risk of making them rebel against the least hint of personal organization.

But let us not exaggerate the possible injury; human beings, especially the young, are remarkably adaptive. Don't they get used to living amid bricks and asphalt and to seeing trees only on trips?

Those who make us wait

THE YOUNG apprentice of time, which we all were, will learn to accept appointments, delays, the cutting up of the day into slices, and a minimum of programming. But nothing guarantees that he will learn to be on time.

How do you explain that in the same family Catherine arrives on time, finishes her projects punctually and seems relaxed, while Jack runs after the minutes, misses the train and always finds excuses to procrastinate? It is not only a question of learning, but also one of personality.

All of us know people who are chronically late so often that we even suspect them of having a psychological problem.

The delayers belong to one of two main groups: the narcissists and the procrastinators. By making you wait the narcissist is making himself or herself desired. Among the narcissists we find those who take forever to put on their makeup or those who can work only under pressure. Creative people often get a high from work done at the last minute. Let us not forget that the delay imposed on others is a mark of power over them. This is the complex of the diva.

To take a famous example, François Mitterand insisted on being the last to arrive at a meeting or a meal. When he risked being on time, he would ask his chauffeur to park around the corner, where he read the newspaper so that he could be late.

The procrastinators suffer from a great inability to make a decision, a condition that is close to being an obsession. In the least serious cases, it makes it difficult to choose what clothes or what dish to order in a restaurant. In an extreme case, decisions are constantly put off. We would do well to avoid a boss who is a procrastinator.

On the other hand, a good relationship with time is one of the signs of a well-balanced personality, one that is sensitive to the needs of others.

The wondrous memory of the present

BECAUSE WE live in societies, we must better practice the art of time. It is crucial to our (better) well-being. Though not ideal, for it would be better not to need rules. We have in fact unlearned a lot since childhood.

It is in our early years that we are most profoundly, naturally, and intimately involved with time.

Never again will we be as open as the child for whom everything is new and who can dream and be surprised and forget everything else to benefit from the moment. Without the burden of a past, without care for the future, we live our childhood happily in the present, before our memories and our projects gnaw it down from both ends.

The fundamental experience of the present, of the fullness of the moment, the intensity of feeling (joy/pain; pleasure/suffering) here and now, is not that difficult to acquire, since it is within reach of every child. What is harder is to not forget it.

This knowledge is decisive, for it is its recollection we will later pursue. Mastering time has in effect two inseparable, although nearly opposite, goals. The most obvious, although not necessarily the most important, is to be more efficient. The most fulfilling and the hardest is to relearn to take advantage of the moment with the intensity we experienced as a six-year-old, when a ray of sunshine warmed us in a pine grove.

These physical impressions of plenitude date from those

early years and often even from our adolescence, and they become a reference for the rest of our life. As for those extensive or expensive efforts we make in the midst of our stressed existence to find some pleasure, it is this quality of the moment which serves as our checkpoint without our knowledge. Many seek to regain the wonders of their innocent years by means of therapy or by an often painful internal search.

Little by little, Westerners have whittled away at the present. To retrieve it, they must undergo a genuine reeducation and must be willing to make some concessions. The philosopher E. M. Cioran said it perfectly: "We can savor the flavor of our days only if we bypass the obligation to have a destiny."

In search of the temporal horizon

THE FARTHER we are from childhood, the more we change our temporal horizon by refining our knowledge of time. This change is one of the most significant and least explored personal parameters.

The temporal horizon is the distance at which we establish spontaneously our vision of the future or the past, the span of time we can consider with ease. It varies greatly from one society to another, depending on the individuals and on their stage in life.

Animals probably do not have a temporal horizon. They live exclusively in the present; they seem incapable of recalling an instant in the past or of anticipating. On the other hand, they have a memory since they recognize places, situations, and people.

Human beings have the fundamental faculty of making use of the past in the present (what we have learned or known) in order to fashion the future (foreseeing, organizing, avoiding danger).

In primitive societies, the temporal horizon may go back far into the past but remains close when considering the future. Everything depends on how we think about time. To think about the future, we must first believe that it exists. Primitive peoples think of time as circular and of the past as necessarily repeating itself. It is enough for them to predict the future by projecting the past into it.

Even today, many underdeveloped countries have a too-near perspective on the future. The famous Spanish *mañana* can mean "tomorrow" as well as "one day" or even "never." In the Middle East, an appointment made more than a week ahead runs the risk of it never occurring because the local temporal horizon and the field of action do not extend much beyond a week.

On the other hand, the characteristic of Western civilization is the tilt of the temporal horizon toward the future at the expense of the past. Americans, with their brief past, were the forerunners. It was they who inculcated ancient Europe with planning, foresight, and scenarios for the future, without which there would have been no Allied landing on the beaches of Normandy in 1944 and no landing on the moon in 1969.

We are paid to see far into the future

IT IS not only societies that have a temporal horizon. Each individual has his or her own, the result of a cluster of educational and genetic factors. Let us look at ours.

Do our memories smother us like heavy bags or do we complain that our memory fails us? Are we apt to look ahead a month or a year in advance, or are we often surprised, when we look at our appointment book, that we have scheduled ourselves an appointment for next week? Do we prefer to organize or to improvise?

In general, most people ponder the past rather than the future, if only because it is easier to remember than to foresee.

Most of the attempts to master time will attempt to improve our relation to the near and to the more distant future.

When we are children, our horizon is very narrow. At first, we know only the present and therefore we know well how to capitalize on it. But everything in our education conspires to enlarge our perspective toward the future by developing a respect for schedules and deadlines (such as exams), as well as toward the past, since education depends on memorization. To study is to form useful memories, from the multiplication table to human rights.

Education pushes our horizon back toward the past. Our professional life does the same for the future. We begin by solving problems from day to day. Then we quickly learn that we need to think further and further ahead if we are to obtain more interesting and more complex assignments. The horizon of a manager is his or her three-year plan, that of a healthcare provider the time it will take to obtain a more advanced accreditation, that of a writer how long it will take her or him to write the next article, or the next book. An employee thinks of the next vacation, paying off her house, the children's college tuition and then their weddings, and finally retirement. The future pulls us forward.

According to the English sociologist Elliott Jaques, the temporal horizon determines everyone's level of compensation. Without supervision, an unskilled worker performs tasks that last up to two hours, a foreman a week, a manager a month, a boss a year. Matsushita, the founder of the Japanese company that bears his name, said that he planned two centuries ahead. The further ahead we plan, the more we are paid. This criterion seems to be transnational: workers in Portugal or in Singapore with the same temporal horizon are likely to be paid an equivalent salary, no matter what their occupation.

The time you need for each thing

THE PROBLEMS we face in relation to time can be quite profound. Not everyone has a feeling for the time needed to do things. In other words, not everyone has a feeling for duration.

We internalize the time needed for certain activities only after much experience with various durations. But even though our life is filled with repetitive activities, even mature and highly educated individuals persist in committing the errors of a beginner.

Thus, one of the leading doctors in New York habitually makes his patients wait between forty-five and ninety minutes. Sometimes the delays reach such alarming proportions that his assistant has to call all the afternoon patients to tell them to come in two hours later than originally scheduled. The diagnosis is simple: the doctor schedules his patients every half hour even though he keeps each one at least three-quarters of an hour. He has been behaving in this manner for years and yet he refuses to recognize the problem.

How many times have we been collared by a visitor who said he wanted to see us for twenty minutes and who, after an hour, is still describing his problem?

The simplest acts of life are not always timed in our head. A woman may in all sincerity claim she needs five minutes to put on her makeup, or a man to shave, while in fact they take twice as long. It is neither common nor particularly pleasant to clock ourselves, but we still need to know the duration of our daily activities. It is with these pieces of time that we construct our days. Several minor errors of judgment piling up create the long delays that end in the guilty phone call: "Don't wait for me for dinner."

Although less frequently, we also see the opposite behavior. People who allow too much time and arrive early for appointments, filling up waiting rooms, arriving at the airport hours before takeoff. These people are merely operating on the basis of different motives.

The more complicated the endeavor, the costlier a poor

appreciation of duration. As in the case of the temporal horizon, those who know how to avoid unnecessary delays stand to gain a substantial bonus.

To each, his or her own time

"ETERNITY IS long. Especially toward the end," said Woody Allen, with his genius for bringing out the obvious through the absurd. The obvious is that our mind cannot imagine eternity, or even a much shorter period. The age of the earth, for example, is more than four billion years. That is clearly a lot, but for our brain what difference is there between forty and four million years?

So we should invent a metaphor, as we do for children, to translate this reality into an image we can understand. If the entire existence of the earth, from its creation until today, were compressed into one year, humans would have appeared only at 11:45 P.M. on December 31. Now we can begin to figure the age of the earth.

In the seventeenth century, the mathematician Blaise Pascal noted that we cannot understand the two infinities, that is, the very small and the very large. A millionth of a second, during which exciting things happen for an elementary particle, leaves us entirely cold.

And to complicate things, our perception of even the most familiar durations can be altered by our emotions. What is shorter than a night of love? Longer than a second when our fingers are jammed in a car door? Our week flies by like a day if we enjoy our work and an hour can drag like a day if we don't.

Perceived time, which is the time we live, varies infinitely depending on our temperament, our life experiences, our age and our experiences. That is why, even though time is unique and each of us has as much of it as does our neighbor, the way we live it and use it is so different and so little dissected. The advantage of this surprising situation is that, once we understand it, we can make many improvements. The most important for each of us is the way in which we make use of our hours and days.

Because the lack of time is caused by the way we make use of it.

You Rediscover Your Time

A hard day for Charles · What is our priority? · Sea lions from morning until night · No sooner said than done · The gang of time-stealers · Our most invincible adversary · Lateness, the sport of the dissatisfied · Why people are overworked · The advantages of a banal neurosis · Five principles by which to live less well

A hard day for Charles

THE MOMENT of truth comes about 7 P.M. Charles, who has been in his office since 10 A.M., tries to remember what he did today. He draws a blank. For a full minute, he cannot recall anything. He is neither ill nor drunk. It is the same almost every evening.

He simply has trouble focusing on a day like a treadmill, during which he was interrupted constantly. How many times? He could not tell. In fact, according to statistics, it was no less than seventy times. And the pile of papers on his desk doesn't make him happy: notes and mail that arrived during the day and that he has not yet read. Nearby, a folder of material for a report that he was to have written today and that he has not even looked at.

He knows he still has a half hour of work to do if he want to at least write the letters that absolutely must be sent the next morning. Then he will go home, with his papers in his briefcase, resigned to tackling the report after dinner.

When his wife sweetly asks what he has done at the office that day, he answers, "Nothing important," and that is the truth.

In the evening he allows himself some wine. According to his doctor, wine is the best natural tranquilizer. He and his wife talk about the trip to Rome they may be able to take in the spring. Then he remembers the folder and does not have the heart for it. He allows himself a few minutes of television, knowing that he will quickly fall asleep. Tomorrow, he promises himself, he will wake up at 6 A.M., feeling refreshed, and begin his report while the family sleeps.

This is a commonplace scene, repeated hundreds of thousands of times a day. Charles will finally write his report, although not as soon nor as well as he had intended. But he will continue to lack time precisely because he does not have time to think about it.

To hear ourselves talk, we are the victims of time and, in fact, the environment is partly responsible. But even when we are pressured by outside forces, some of us try to improve the situation while others do not know how to tackle the problem.

Without our knowing it, it is we who deprive ourselves of a great deal of time because of our routine, a guilty conscience, or simply a lack of thought.

What is our priority?

WHETHER AT work or at home, we have many tasks that must be done. Small or large, these are the activities that make up our days. But it is we who, in principle, choose the order in which they are done and decide on their priority.

In fact, we usually do the following:

What we enjoy doing before what we dislike
What we can do quickly before what takes time
What is easy before what is difficult
What we know how to do before what is new
What is urgent before what is important
What others ask us to do before what we ourselves choose

That is not all. What is written down on our calendar for a given hour takes precedence over unscheduled work. We are often more available to those who interrupt us than for our own priorities. Similarly, we tend to deal with problems in the order in which they appear, which may not be the order of their importance.

When several people depend on us—clients, subordinates, children—we deal first with those who are the most vocal in their demands, even if their problems are not necessarily the most urgent.

It is not surprising that these reflexes become habits and that Charles does not get to his report until the very last minute.

There is no need to emphasize that this list of attitudes, which all of us recognize at least in part, enumerates everything that should be avoided if we are to use our time better. But this is how we have acted since we began school and that, burdened with work, we have not had the opportunity to change except for the worse. The next question is obvious: why do we behave in this way?

Sea lions from morning until night

LET US begin with the law of least effort. We are well aware that within many a workaholic there lurks a lazy child who quickly learned to avoid any additional work by giving the impression, even to himself, of doing tons of it! A ten- to twelve-hour day provides him or her with an unassailable cover. Who would dare peek at what is actually going on? An extreme case is that of the well-known advertising man who is the last to arrive at the dinners he hosts. He makes himself more important in his own eyes by choosing to appear overworked rather than polite.

Even though we may all have our secret share of heedlessness, that cannot be the whole explanation. Industrial societies were not built by slackers. Other psychological mechanisms must be at work.

Many people find it hard every morning to get back to work, to find once again the right rhythm. The first thing they do when they get to work is to go to the coffee machine. Then they begin with small tasks, neither too long nor too hard, make a few telephone calls, read a couple of e-mails. After that, they swear, they will get to the important work.

But before these small victories are won, other people attack. By means of phone calls, interruptions, faxes, e-mails, they send us balls we are (well) trained to catch on the tips of our noses.

And so passes another day in which we play at being sea lions until the evening.

Today again, we were unable to get to the more important work because of the interrupters who sabotaged the least stretch of time that would have allowed us to make a more sustained effort. Luckily, every so often we are left in peace for a short while. With time at our disposal, we promise ourselves that we will finally be able to get some work done.

The trouble is, of course, that all the days end up looking alike because we have ourselves made no changes in our routines.

No sooner said than done

THE BRAIN IS the least used part of our body during our lifetime. A day full of activity, even intense activity, saps our energy, wears on our nerves, but demands little of our cortex. Most of our daily work holds nothing new for us. Activities such as creation, originality, and invention, which would put our neurons to work, are rather rare. Let us be honest and admit that an average number of ideas, a little experience, and a minimum of common sense are enough to deal with most situations.

To go from routine thinking to real concentration is like jumping from a slow moving-sidewalk to a faster one. We have to concentrate our energy and flexibility in order to make the leap. This is one of the reasons, although not the only one, that we rarely think about the way we use time, even if it is the cause of our suffering.

We spend our days doing various undemanding tasks but we prefer not to change our pattern. And when we take on work that demands sustained thought, three telephone calls are enough to waylay us for another day.

The fractionalization of modern time and the proliferation of our activities have shortened these pauses, these disengagements, to the point where they have completely disappeared. Appointments, meetings, and telephone calls are chained together with no transition. And the worst is that we end up liking it.

Quick and jerky actions, balls thrown at us by others stimulate our adrenaline and cause a mini-euphoria. It does not take much to make us feel busy and therefore important. Even if we complain that this way of life is absurd, we are not about to seriously question it.

"The men and women in the technological society have done away with the respites necessary to the rhythm of life," writes Jacques Ellul. "These respites needed to make choices, adapt, and collect ourselves no longer exist.

The rule of life has become: "No sooner said than done."

The gang of time-stealers

NEITHER ALTOGETHER lazy nor truly superficial, nor totally stupid, we are all prone to the misuse of time. It is when these misuses become habits, without our realizing it, that they throw all of our time out of kilter.

Studies have been done for decades, especially in the United States, to list the "time-stealers" to which we are continually exposed. They are the same everywhere.

In the 1970s a researcher, Alec McKenzie, asked various groups of managers to list their time-stealers. He interviewed 40 Canadian colonels, 30 American university presidents, 25 heads of Mexican companies, insurance brokers, African American clergymen, and German managers. Their lists were practically interchangeable.

The external thieves:
  Unexpected or needlessly long phone calls
  Colleagues who stop by to talk about their problems or
    to chat
  Open door policies, the duty to be available
  Visitors, clients, suppliers arriving unexpectedly
  Poorly trained personnel (especially assistants)
  The boss, or even worse, more than one boss
  Business lunches, cocktail parties, and other entertainment for visitors
  Too frequent, too long, or poorly prepared meetings
  Administrative or personal calls
  Upkeep and repair of malfunctioning machines (cars,

computers, television, audio equipment)

Appointments (doctors, music lessons, sports) for the children to which they must be driven

Housework, errands, cooking

Interruptions by children (or parents)

The internal thieves:

Confused or changing priorities and goals

Absence of a daily work plan

Unfinished work or work in progress

Absence of self-imposed deadlines

Tendency to do too much, perfectionism

Lack of order, poorly organized office

Confusing and overlapping responsibilities

Insufficient delegation

Excessive attention to details

Delay in settling conflicts

Resistance to change

Scattered and excessive interests

Inability to say no

Lack of information or insufficient (or excessive) information

Indecision, or decisions made too rapidly (or made by a committee)

Fatigue, being out of shape

There is no point in giving examples of each of these. We recognize in this list those culprits that are part of our lives. The question then is: which are the bigger robbers, the external or the internal thieves?

Peter Drucker, the management guru, performed an enlightening experiment. He made a movie showing a CEO piling on during his day every sin imaginable against the good use of his time and that of his employees.

He asked forty managers for their own list of time-stealers before seeing the film. Most of them accused the "external" thieves. Then he asked them to do the same thing after seeing the film. Most of the thieves became "internal" ones.

If we are honest with ourselves, we will realize as we reread the list of external thieves that most of them are internal thieves in disguise. For the most part they are the handmaidens of the two greater internal thieves: the inability to say no, which buries us in visits, long and useless phone calls, meaningless outings, fatigue, nonessential tasks, and flimsy obligations; and insufficient delegation, which prevents us from sparing ourselves a host of professional and familial tasks that could be done by others or organized in a different way.

Of course, not all constraints are spurious. There are emergencies (but how many of these are real emergencies? remarked a doctor friend). And, in principle, those for whom we work have the right to interrupt us at any time.

How then do we organize ourselves in spite of the unpredictable?

Our most invincible adversary

ALL THESE remarks add up to both bad news and good news. The bad news is that few people are to blame. The good news is that we are in charge and that we have considerable room to maneuver.

Our journey seems to have brought us before a door we will have to open: our own. Like the compass needle pointing north, the needle of time, whatever detours we take, points in one direction only: toward ourselves, with whom the problem begins and ends.

Of course, the period in which we live makes our life complicated and often the behavior of others is not helpful. We would be justified in suing society and our peers for the erosion of our capital of time. But would we have any chance of winning our case?

These facts are as immutable as time. We cannot change them but we can adjust to them, even take advantage of them. Let us remind ourselves (not for the last time) of two facts:

Time passes without stopping. We can lose time but we cannot gain time.
We can only make better use of it.
When we master time, from start to finish, we master ourselves.

All of us began life with the instinctive and self-protective notion that adversity comes from outside. "I didn't do it, he did it," say all children. Forty years later, some keep saying the same thing.

But, having lived and overcome certain obstacles, we begin to realize a more efficacious truth (could this be maturity?); the toughest enemy, the hardest to conquer, the one for whom we make every allowance, is ourself.

Before attacking this adversary methodically and tactfully we must examine his weaknesses. Each of us will perform the examination in his or her own way, but an analysis of some common cases may suggest some ideas and permit comparisons.

For example, if we continue to tolerate these losses of time that we bemoan loudly, is it not because they serve our needs, even if we do not admit it?

Lateness, the sport of the dissatisfied

LET US observe Claire who is always late. She finally arrives at the meeting where everyone is already seated. She comes in, apologizes loudly, disturbs a whole row in reaching her seat, spreads out her things, apologizes again, and even has the nerve to add without laughing: "Go on, please, don't pay attention to me."

And here is Steve, packing his suitcase at the last minute. He fills the house with shouts: "Where are my brown shoes?" and mobilizes the entire family terrified that he will miss his plane.

These games must pay off by attracting attention, getting noticed. Rather than earning praise by great deeds or remarkable findings, people prefer to be the target of negative attention—what a pest!—rather than no attention at all. When parents are indifferent, every child instinctively knows the kind of behavior that is sure to bring back the spotlight.

The laggard would rather create an artificial high than experience no excitement at all.

In a rather dull life we create some excitement for ourselves by playing at the game: "Will I or won't I make my plane?" (and forget my toothbrush?), in the same way too many adolescents play at: "Will I kill myself on my motorcycle?"

And finally, the least important person in a group can, if only for a moment, create the impression of controlling it. By keeping others from beginning—or leaving, speaking, or eating—when they want to, he confers on himself a scrap of the power he fears he lacks.

Many creative people cannot begin work until the very last minute. Only a sense of urgency and the fear of missing an absolute deadline can overcome their enormous anxiety.

If punctuality is the courtesy of kings, tardiness may become the sport of the dissatisfied.

Why people are overworked

The overworked individual also has his reasons for maintaining the situation he complains about.

Men often take on this role in order to avoid most household chores, and it works for them. It may also allow them to avoid for years being responsive to their own children.

At work, Mark faces every unpleasant problem with a furrowed brow. The problem may take care of itself, he hopes, if he doesn't have time to devote to it. And in fact that is what happens more or less in one-third of the cases.

Managers who fear face-to-face confrontations with their employees also play this role. They cannot ever find the time to explain what isn't working. This is also true for politicians who cannot bear to look over the financing of their activities and who will always find something more urgent that has to be dealt with. A miracle, they hope, will allow them to avoid such an examination.

The overworked individual especially seeks to avoid responsibility, intimacy, and well-being.

Responsibility is never far from guilt. The minute we show the slightest aptitude for solving problems, our superiors, colleagues, subordinates, mates, children, and friends vie with each other in proposing new ones. Obligations grab onto our backs like baby possums.

To preserve our vital space-time, we have to be able to refuse without wounding. The alibi works well in two ways which each of us uses according to his temperament: "I can't" and "I don't know how."

The "I can't," or rather "I no longer can," is the prerogative of the strong and credible who we readily concede are already doing a lot. A sign, eyes turned skyward, a few words make it clear that our hero is at the end of his rope and that it would be ungracious to insist.

The "I don't know" is preferred by people who find that pleading definite ineptitude is more effective (and radical). Their balance sheet of time is so obviously disastrous, their delays, their omissions, their defects so obvious and so often repeated that no one would be so foolish as to entrust them with the slightest responsibility. This strategy is not ego-building but it works.

The advantages of a banal neurosis

A LACK of time is also a convenient barrier to intimacy and allows us to avoid others. Over time, two aspects of the life of a couple, sexuality and communication, become threatening to some. They no longer feel able to respond to the needs of the other or, for whatever reason, no longer wish to.

Overwork can be a cause as well as a pretext in the case of sexuality. The decline in libido of the overworked manager is the daily bread of sex therapists.

The office with the lights on late in the evening often shelters a man or woman who finds good reasons for not going home. And at home, tiredness will conveniently excuse his or her silence at the table and the need to fall asleep as soon as possible.

It is an effective technique and hard to criticize. It allows some couples to avoid discussing any sensitive subject for years—that is, if they hold on that long.

Finally, resistance to mastering time may feed on a banal neurosis: the fear of well-being. People suffering from something always talk of getting rid of it, but if the opportunity arises, they do not seize it. That would be too simple.

The guilt inherent in our Judeo-Christian morality makes some of us believe that a portion of discomfort guarantees against worse yet. If everything were going well, fate might avenge itself by striking harder. Hamlet spoke of "The undiscovered country . . . [that] makes us rather bear the ills we have,/Than fly to others we know not of."

And then time etches our features, digs lines in our foreheads, and he or she who has taken on the role of the overworked is not always ready to shed it. What would replace it? What else would define him or her? When we are faced with the choice of remaining stressed and asking fundamental questions about ourselves and the meaning of life, the answer is not always obvious.

This sense of guilt is often unconscious and is intimately linked to our relation to time. We cannot analyze time, understand it, act upon it, if we do not succeed in identifying these messages internalized in childhood.

Often we feel that it is unacceptable to take time for ourselves until the needs of others have been met; in other words, never.

Five principles by which to live less well

A PSYCHOLOGIST, Dr. Alfred Kahler, has identified five principles which, often unconsciously, are at the basis of our actions: hurry up, be perfect, please me, try again, be strong. Five simple recipes that can poison our lives.

Those who "hurry up" think that something that can be done in a leisurely way cannot be important. They need haste to feel justified. So it is enough for them to do things at the last minute and then to complain loudly that they are feeling stressed. Those who want to "be perfect" cannot stop tinkering with the last details. They lose time tidying, refining, controlling, securing. They have trouble deciding for fear their information is not complete. Their perfectionism slows them down and keeps them from having a detached perspective on their work.

Those who want to "please" often say yes when they mean no and find themselves committed to activities that do not interest them. They do not like giving bad news, which keeps them from dealing with situations that are deteriorating. They fear making their goals and intentions known. They are dismayed by broken commitments, but their conscience is at peace because they had wanted to please.

Those who like to "try again" are convinced the task must be hard. They will not take a problem seriously unless it is difficult. The effort rather than the result is their justification. For them, it is less important to accomplish the task than to feel that they have done everything in their power . . . and hardly had any sleep.

Those who want to "be strong" need no one. They must find answers by themselves and do not know how to delegate. They admit to no weaknesses and do not complain. They take on a task, maintain a stiff upper lip, and insist on having been right. Standing ramrod straight on the deck, they will go down with the ship.

Are these the results of parental intimidation, family examples, the influence of educators? It is hard for us to know why we adopt certain dysfunctional attitudes. But these are only a few examples of the infinite number of obstacles that prevent us from making good use of our time. Each of us can fill this zoo with his or her own specimens. If we wish to free ourselves from these abstract principles, we need only remember the diplomat Charles de Talleyrand's advice: "Always lean on principles. They will end up bending."

You Can Master Your Time

Three steps to mastering time

BEFORE AN inalterable, irreversible, and indifferent time, we poor souls still dream of mastering it. Are we mad or absurdly pretentious?

Is it a question of mastering time the way a cowboy takes control of his horse after he has been thrown a dozen times? Not at all. In the rodeo, the strength of the horse is balanced by the tenacity of the rider. *Not only are we the weaker party against time but we have no control whatsoever over it, as we have no control over our need to take in oxygen at every moment of our life.*

What we call mastery of time for convenience (or are we simply boasting?) is only mastery of ourselves in relation to time. The horse we are riding will never stop or slow down. Still we cannot get off. But there should be a way of not letting ourselves be dragged or tossed around. We should be able to right ourselves and begin to match the horse's gait and sometimes even overtake it.

But are we even capable of mastery? Well, yes, we have mastered the driving of a car. Do you remember when . . .

At first, never having even touched a wheel, we were at once eager and frightened. It seemed so complicated and we wondered how we would ever be able to drive with ease at more than sixty miles an hour while at the same time chatting pleasantly or thinking about something else.

After a few lessons we were convinced that we would never be able to let the clutch out, engage the right gear, use the turn signal and look in the rearview mirror, all this simultaneously, before making a turn. Until the day when, in fact, we drove with ease at more than sixty miles an hour while chatting. And that is precisely what happened when we had stopped thinking about it. We had mastered driving.

Mastery over any new activity proceeds through three stages: first, the motivation to reach a desired goal; then, the will to overcome disorientation and discouragement; and finally, complete internalization. We can then concentrate, not on mastery itself, which is now ours, but on what we can achieve because of it.

Mastery is the sister of elegance

WHAT IS a master and what can we expect from mastery?

Consider master Ueshiba as he practices Aikido. For many minutes, this smiling little seventy-five-year-old is set upon by some strapping young men who, alone or in a group, try to throw him off balance; he seems content to move his arms around, to outline some feints. But suddenly the young men are literally thrown into the distance. The effort was small but the effect was great.

Listen to Isaac Stern as he demonstrates proper bowing technique to his attentive Chinese students. Relaxed, joking with his audience, he nevertheless draws from his violin sounds that can make you weep. Or the surgeon working in a small and modestly equipped hospital who is asked how he manages to get the best results in the region in asepsis and scarring. His reply? "I know exactly where I have to make the incision."

Precision, economy of means, and a near absence of effort: mastery is the sister of elegance.

Through mastery we succeed in overcoming a problem that until then dominated us, through knowledge, training and, most of all, because we feel confident we can find solutions. Self-assured and well-trained, we finally achieve a state that marks the essence of mastery: we are able to apply just the right amount of energy at the right spot. In mastery we find one of our richest sources of internal satisfaction.

Each kind of mastery is accompanied by an appreciable gain of time. It is better to have worked through a new recipe before serving a new dish to guests. When all remains to be discovered, everything takes a long time. But after the fifth try, the time is reduced to a third.

"To be a professional" boils down to doing better and faster than those who do not.

How is it done?

WHAT IS mastery of time if not knowing how to fit in it, move in it, rely on it, use it, and enjoy it? Time itself does not move; we live in it and give it shape by our actions and our movements. Often, we imprison ourselves by the way we spin out our time, because we weave this web daily by the choices we make. We can only influence the design to fit us and decrease the sense that we have been trapped.

In our daily life, how do we recognize those who have mastered time? Whom do we admire or secretly envy?

The doctor who behaves as if we were her only patient of the day. We have confidence in him because he gives us his entire attention, listens to us, and never looks at his watch.

The friend living abroad whom we telephone on our arrival, who meets us right away, spends the evening with us, and takes us back to the airport. Secretly we think that if he had descended on us unexpectedly, he would have upset all our plans and we would have been annoyed that she had not forewarned us.

The mother (ours?) who is always available to her children and who can at the same time prepare delicious meals, take good care of her looks, and still radiate good humor.

The woman with the demanding job and a healthy marriage who every day travels across town to visit her ailing father in the hospital.

The boss who sees you within a day of your request, without hiding behind a schedule you know to be full, and speaks to you without the least evidence of tension.

Everyone who leads a varied life (at a professional, emotional, familial, interior, and physical level) without visibly sacrificing any part of it.

In addition to constant serenity, availability to others, and multiple interests, the real masters, because they have perspective, also have humor.

Can I trust myself?

But we are not there yet. We need to identify and then overcome four obstacles:

1. We do not know ourselves well enough.
2. We do not understand time well enough.
3. We allow ourselves to be encumbered by ourselves and by others.
4. We do not think enough about the use we make of our time.

The seventeenth-century Dutch prince, William of Orange, noted that "There are no favorable winds for the one who does not know where he is going." In the same way, he who does not know himself cannot achieve mastery. But few of us can state clearly what we want in life, what gives us pleasure, what we are capable of, what our weaknesses are, etc.

To make better use of our time it is not absolutely necessary to understand ourselves completely; that would be asking too much. But we should be at least aware of what in us can make it hard to reach this goal. In this respect, we already have some resources.

No one knows better than we do how far we can be trusted. No one has suffered more from our defects, been tricked more often by us, or been as deceived by us than we ourselves.

Each of us has some ideas of his or her lapses, of the ways we drift off course. At the beginning of the book, I list some the reader may not have thought of. Mastery implies that we "do with." Let us begin by making an honest inventory of these lapses. Later we will see how to make the best use of these.

Next we must be clear about the reasons for wanting to work toward mastery: Is it to become more efficient or to suffer less from our failures? To discard the feeling of always being stressed or to inspire confidence in others? To begin a new project or to have more time for sleep? Or, simply, to live better?

We cannot get a handle on our time unless we know what we want to do with it, generally and specifically, in the final analysis or in stages.

A poor education

WE NEED not be ashamed that we know so little about time; no one has ever talked to us about it.

On the other hand, we are well acquainted with money, its status, its publicity, its champions and its dedicated servants, its indices, and the honors it confers. A tag indicates the monetary value of the smallest object. But have we ever seen it written on the back of a book: "$25/200 minutes"?

The value of time is not taught except to those who are paid by the hour and who, when they begin to work, must be instructed to be on time or to keep accurate records of how they spend their time.

The two activities in our daily lives in which time visibly reigns are cooking—the time it takes to cook food—and sports—clocked time. But in each case we are interested only in how long it takes, in the duration, not in what it feels like.

No one has ever taught us to observe the way we use time throughout our day or in executing a project. No one has ever asked us to keep track of the time it takes us to go through our daily lives and to think about ways we could be less burdened. Has anyone ever told us that the order in which we do things is important and may affect the time it takes us to do something and even how much we enjoy doing it?

Most of our stresses and slippages are caused by a mistaken understanding of time, in the same way that inattention to delays is the cause of overwork and of many disappointments.

We have even been led to believe that the nature of time changes when we leave work and that we could treat it differently. Whether or not we choose to change our disposition or attitude when we leave work for home is a personal choice. But to pretend that in doing so the texture and speed of time change is a source of a string of errors.

Mastery of time is not a sporadic attitude. Either it applies to all twenty-four hours of the day or it is only a snare.

As if we could follow a diet at lunch but not at dinner.

If you had been taught this lesson at the right time, would you be reading this book now?

A thorough housecleaning in our head

IT IS critical that we understand in concrete ways how we clutter our time senselessly. We must clean house.

At home, each room, each piece of furniture is covered with objects, useless pieces of paper, and dust-catchers we have forgotten because we see them all the time. If, one day, it occurs to us to take a fresh look at everything, the unwanted objects are either tossed into the garbage immediately and without guilt or relegated to the attic. Similarly, our time is littered with routines and chores we can eliminate.

Since these routines are not as easily spotted as objects, we will look closely at ways of identifying them before getting rid of them. Let us note at the outset that they come from three sources: from other people, from ourselves, and more particularly, from our memory.

"Others": they are the cause of an impressive list of "yeses" that should have been "nos"—not always because we are weak or kind, but often because we do not think—and which add up to hours and days lost for no reason.

"Ourselves": everything we do through habit, such as tidying up every day or maintenance that could be done once or twice a week.

A special place should be made for clearing our memory.

Trying to remember everything is as brave and as useless as walking up ten flights of stairs when there is an elevator: It is good exercise but not smart when you are in a hurry.

You may be familiar with the following anecdote: When someone asked Einstein his telephone number, he looked in the phone book, explaining that it was useless to remember numbers that one could easily look up. This little story is pertinent as we are told that everything we need to know will soon be available on the Internet.

More than knowledge and attitude, mastery is a practice. Hence the need to begin by examining the use we make of our time—hourly, daily, weekly, monthly, annually, and existentially.

A philosophy of life

EVEN WITHOUT a diploma, a master of her time can expect some important rewards:

- ❖ She knows at every moment what use she wants to make of her time.
- ❖ She knows her weaknesses and her failings and has learned to outwit them.
- ❖ She has evaluated the time she spends on each act or phase of her life.
- ❖ She lives just one time—professional or personal, routine or unusual—her own.
- ❖ She frees her memory of the "what" in favor of the "how" and the "why," because she has memory aids that allow her to forget nothing.
- ❖ She considers every day the use of her time in relation to a clear set of goals.

It is certainly not enough to write down this list nor even to learn it by heart. Only the strongly motivated can undertake this quasi reeducation.

Motivation comes first, because you cannot undertake such a project without the reassurance that comes from a clear vision of its benefits.

The mastery of time is not only a weapon against stress, it is also a philosophy of life.

We all recognize that, along with health, time is our only real wealth, the coin into which we convert all our life experiences. Not paying too much, not spending foolishly, not wasting our irreplaceable capital: these management notions become less abstract when we recognize that it is a question of life.

We are well aware that money is nothing in relation to time. When justice wants to punish, a fine and a foreclosure seem trivial. We dread only the punishments like prison that deprive us of our time of freedom. The most barbaric, the death penalty, is the one punishment that in a single blow does away with all remaining time.

Because time is the very fabric of our life, a mastery over time should be of the highest priority. Who would willingly waste his life, even a little of it?

Management is not the same as mastery

THE EMPEROR Titus, a liberal who built the Coliseum in Rome in the first century, was in the habit of asking himself every evening: "Did I make good use of my time?" Those who do the same feel satisfied when their day has unfolded harmoniously, without waste and in conformity with their goals or expectations.

On the other hand, we are ill at ease when, in response to the same question, we think of all the unproductive waiting, the continual interruptions, the missed deadlines, the rushing about that makes us feel as bruised as if we had tumbled down a hill.

There is a fundamental difference between mastery and management of time. The goal of the second, which is the subject of a great number of books and seminars, especially in the United States, is to gain "an hour a day" or "to accomplish more in the same day." But efficiency is only part of our problem of time.

We aspire to master our time not only to gain time but because we want to live better.

As we progress toward mastery, we fashion ourselves, we think about the way we live, and each of us reaches conclusions useful to him or her. The process is thus more profound and more fruitful than just an improvement in performance.

The control and management of our time allows us to achieve a sequence of events that is better coordinated but does not ensure the essential, which is a total vision, even (we can dream) a new meaning. So it is natural to link this quest for mastery to certain principles basic to Oriental thought: "The goal is less important than the way." In other words, the result is less important than the means to obtain it. "We can dominate only that from which we have some distance," a maxim that is more applicable every day. What lives within us, what obsesses us has a hold on us. We are the prisoners of rage, passion, or simply annoyance as long as we are unable to say: "I feel the rage, but I am not this rage, and therefore I could just as well not feel it in a while."

We must experience this distancing, this de-identification with something that bothers us in order to understand the nature of the difficulty, a process necessary to all mastery.

Who is a master of time?

THE PERSON who has mastered time can appear to be a flawless programmer, a skilled calculator, a meticulous organizer ready for anything and everything. That would not be too bad.

But I prefer to see him as a thinker, attentive and smiling, who mentally dances from one moment to another.

She is a good judge of herself and of reality, has a keen sense of the passing moment, knows how to take advantage of it (and may also suffer from it), but adapts quickly. She knows how to alternate periods of intensity and dreaminess, because she knows full well the value of transitions. Change is her element and helps her exist for she no longer fears it. Everyone marvels at her accessibility, some may even ask if she is underemployed. She knows it and it makes her smile. Time for this person is flexible.

You can invent another image more to your liking, an image that will be most useful to sustain you as you begin a path that will not always be easy, because the real world rarely allows one to achieve complete mastery. It is useful to describe it here as a goal, a point of reference, but the real world has its share of constraints.

To master one's time, one learns that one must first be master of oneself, without a boss, without subordinates, even without a family. But we are not starting from zero, which brings up the objection: "All this is only for the well-off. It does not apply to me."

But maybe this is an excuse to avoid trying. None of our lives is ideal and each one of us needs to improve. A little, a lot, totally? That will depend less on the individual's specific circumstances than on the energy we are prepared to invest in changing.

We return again to the question of motivation, which, more than discipline, is in the modern world "the main force of armies." The time has come to explore ways of finding and above all preserving the motivation we need to make these changes.

Organized, but free

"WHAT?! I'M struggling to keep up with demands that fill my life and you want me to add others?" This objection is hurled at us any time we make an attempt at mastery (of the body, of oneself, of time).

Again, a comparison with dieting is illuminating. People diet because they do not feel good about themselves and they don't like what they see in the mirror. But if they seem heavy in their own eyes, it is because every day they chose small immediate gratifications (another bite) rather than the long-term satisfaction of feeling good about themselves.

A new diet consists of giving up these gratifications right away and for a long time. For a period of time we must bear the inconvenience of a corpulence that does not disappear right away. We must agree wholeheartedly to a period of austerity for the sake of a probable goal that we desire but that we will attain only in the future.

It cannot be easy because failures are numerous. To find the strength to diet, the situation must either have become unbearable or the required asceticism must find its compensation in other realms (the young woman in love begins to lose weight if her sexual life has become more gratifying than her meals).

The transition from a painful and tense situation to a state of serenity through mastery is more efficient. The bad news is that at the beginning one must endure a period of greater constraint. But the good news is that the results can be achieved much faster than in dieting.

This reminds me of something that happened to me. After I had lost twenty pounds, people kept on asking me: "Why are you dieting? You're already very thin!" They were taken aback by the simplicity of my answer: "But it is *because* I am dieting that I am thin!" These are the same people who ask me: "Where does someone as hyperorganized as you find the time to live?" and who are skeptical when I tell them: "It is *since* I became organized that I have more time to live."

Freedom is no longer bought with a gun: it comes from organization. Can you imagine a more appealing motive than freedom?

GIVE YOURSELF TIME

Getting ahead of the event

AT THE starting line of the Olympic slalom, the contestants are silently waiting for the event to begin. Their helmets and glasses hide their faces. Their arms are folded in front of them and their right hands outline in a curving gesture the path they will follow around the poles. Their eyes closed, they review internally the slope where everything will be played out in less than two minutes.

Just before taking off for the slope, these expert skiers go over the whole trail. They review the course they will have to follow without having time to think. This preparatory concentration is vital if they are to perform at their peak.

Similarly, all of us have mentally gone over the arguments, the essential points, the possible pitfalls the night before a delicate conversation, a speech, or an exam.

When we enter a critical or dangerous phase of our life, the unknown frightens us. To tame it, we try to imagine it ahead of time and to anticipate the possible situations in which we will find ourselves as well as our responses and reactions.

Unfortunately, all too often what ought to be concentration turns into anxiety. And generally we go through this exercise only on exceptional occasions whereas it could become a very useful tool in our daily work. For while we cannot change the course of time, we have a major trump card: *thanks to our brain, by anticipating the event, we can overtake it. And we are the only living beings who are capable of this achievement.*

The art of time lies in being able to exploit this trump card. Haven't we often regretted that we did not anticipate consequences that, had we but thought a little, were entirely predictable?

Wanting, then choosing

IN ORDER to take advantage of the power that our imagination gives us, we must activate three separate human capabilities: the power to predict (in a month I will leave for San Diego); the ability to will (I will take advantage of this trip to surf); and the ability to prepare ourselves (I'm not in shape, so I'll start working on my equilibrium on a skateboard).

In a complex society, everyone must be able to predict, otherwise we won't get a seat on the plane, there will be no money at the end of the month and nothing in the refrigerator at dinnertime. This ability to program, which is not very original, at the minimum involves an appointment book and it can always be improved. Everyone can do it and it makes life more pleasant.

Volition is in general more difficult to express clearly. We think we know what we want but when we look at it closely, it may turn out to be rather vague.

Anticipation, which should be the logical outcome of prediction and volition, is the prerogative of only a minority, for going from thought to act seems difficult for most of us.

We need to examine why we make so little use of our remarkable ability to create and plan. All attempts to regain control over our time begin with such a clear-eyed examination.

We should be free and decisive, but we seem to be at the mercy of pressures (to find a job or a house), of drives (to get married or have children), or of external stimuli (to consume) that are enough to occupy most of us and to give us the comforting feeling that we are always thinking of new projects. But are these projects really ours? Did we choose them and do they occupy our minds? When we ask these questions point-blank, we find evasive answers.

Mastery of time remains an illusion if we do not constantly manifest our will and if our goals are not clear. Our mastery is then reduced to tricks of time management, such as making better use of the telephone and avoiding overlong meetings.

We have more projects than we have time to execute them. We must therefore structure our time around our objectives because the art of time, like the art of governing, consists of making the right choices.

What do I do now?

A BRITISH humorist once said that the only important question in life is: "What do I do next?" We ask this question constantly. "Should I get up? What should I wear? Whom shall I call? Isn't it time to talk about something else? Will I ask a question? Should I insist? What are we doing this evening? What time will I go home?" Do, do, do. Our life is a series of acts connected by the answers we give to these mixes of questions, often without a thought.

Even if action is natural to us—even those who call themselves lazy can rarely tolerate real inaction—we prefer a predictable answer to "What do I do now." In short, we are creatures of habit even if we think otherwise. We take comfort in automatic choice (brush our teeth, go to work) whereas a real decision, which involves novelty, seems tiring and easy to evade.

Action has a philosophical dimension. We exist and we are sure we exist only through the actions we choose that are original, different, and inventive—in short innovative and all our own. They create for us an existence in the eyes of others and engender in us an indispensable feeling of vitality.

There is nothing original about acting; everyone does it. When we run into someone we know, we are never asked "Who are you?" but rather "What are you doing?" In the answer to this "what" lies the difference between us and others. Our projects are therefore crucial because they allow us to transcend a simple routine or a quasi-automatic reaction to the demands of our surroundings.

Using our time better makes sense only if we transform it into projects—including the project to do nothing at certain times—that give time its real meaning. And our projects are expressed in goals that are also prioritized.

These goals not only help us to plan our activities but give them meaning and make it possible for us to measure the results.

My goals, or those of others?

BEFORE WE begin the process of establishing goals, let us make sure they are ours and not those of others. Some of our goals are inherited directly from our parents, some come from the organization we belong to, some we acquire from our loved ones and people we respect. Is there room left for our own legitimate demands?

Legitimate? Not everyone believes we have the right to have our own goals. The Judeo-Christian culture in which most of us have been brought up subtly preaches self-effacement. And adopting the goals of others relieves us of the need to ask questions about ourselves that are too searching. It follows that any attempt at living better presupposes a minimum of temperate egoism. Some have nothing to prove in this area, others will have to try a little harder to assert themselves.

Try this simple concrete exercise: examine your schedule, your normal way of functioning, and separate the activities you have chosen freely from those that are responses to the demands of your professional or familial surroundings.

It is very instructive to review the way we use our time while asking ourselves at each step: "Did I really want to do this?"

But be careful. Don't try to look like a martyr and exaggerate your sacrifices. Except for those who suffer from a persecution complex, we share with others a certain tendency toward hedonism, even though it is rarely made explicit. Two thousand five hundred years ago, Buddha already stated that man's first duty was to avoid suffering.

Twenty-five centuries later, the biologist Henri Laborit, on the basis of his experiments and an analysis of the structure of the brain, declared: "Everything we do is in pursuit of pleasure," or, at the very least, the avoidance of displeasure.

Let us admit we have a right to pleasure

WE ACCEPT the right to pleasure with difficulty because our collective unconscious still sees it in disrepute. What would we think of someone who said: "For me, the only goal in life is pleasure"? An egoist, an affected hedonist? In fact the only difference between him and us, insists Laborit, is that he says it out loud, whereas we do it without saying it or, rather, without realizing it.

But I spend a good part of my days doing things I'd rather not do.

That is true. But these are things that give you the means to do what does give you pleasure; and they also allow you to avoid the greater displeasure of being unemployed.

Maybe. But there are some things I do out of a sense of duty to my family and friends. They bring me nothing but trouble.

I'm not sure. What about the merit you acquire in your own eyes and in those of others? That is an essential pleasure.

What about the masochists who hurt themselves?

Exactly. They like it.

What about suicide? That is certainly not done for pleasure.

It is, in a way. Don't we do it to end a suffering that we believe, rightly or wrongly, to be worse than death?

We introduce the principle of pleasure or nonsuffering at the beginning of our discussion of the goals of life in order to shed a little more light on ourselves. What if there were no altruists at all but only egoists whose personal programming led them to find pleasure in pleasing others?

And what if our "duties" were either the proof we need to feel that we are "worthy" or useless constraints we have not yet had the courage to shed? The Buddhists' message, like that of Laborit and of many others, is one of joyous modesty.

Let us not make ourselves more deserving than we are, *and let us admit our desire to succeed in life, for it is certain that no one else will do it for us.*

The project to live better

ISN'T LIVING better the best of all projects? Just improving our work performance is not enough for us if we are sufficiently motivated to perfect ourselves in the art of time. A bonus of an improved quality of personal life seems indispensable. In that reality, everyone can find rewarding goals.

Let us take a look at the parts of our private, personal life that are truly ours, those for which we say we lack time. Isn't now the right time to make some corrective changes? For each of the following points mentioned below, let us ask four questions: "Does it concern me? Where am I in respect to it today? Where do I want to go from here? In what length of time?"

Time for the body

WE DO not care much about our body before the age of twenty-five, unless we are naturally athletic. Our youth takes care of it; we will worry about it later. After the age of twenty-five we are so involved with building a career and/or a family that the only time we devote to our body is when we sleep, which we never seem to do enough.

After thirty-five, on this kind of schedule, we have acquired some bad habits and every new year we resolve—this time, we swear we will do it—to do something about it.

As time passes, it is harder to catch up. But our body is the receiver and becomes the amplifier of all our sensations, that is, our pleasures, from the simplest, such as breathing the morning air or the smell of bread baking to the most complex, such as our sexuality. The more in shape we are, the more intense and the deeper is our pleasure.

And what is more, we expect to live longer than our parents; we must then not only keep on living, but also feel well as long as possible.

Maintenance, exercise, grooming, all these take time; but aren't they a natural priority?

Distractions and pleasures

Leisure time

Besides television (but why not? everyone will soon have a channel to her or his taste) we all have our favorite leisure-time activities. The ballet? Dinner with friends? Rock concerts? Basketball games? The latest best-seller?

Do we still know how to enjoy ourselves, or have we forgotten what we enjoyed when we were eighteen?

It is too tiring to go to bed late, going out without the children is complicated and expensive, and if we are part of a couple, our mate's likes may not be the same as ours.

So . . . television? But we keep on falling asleep in front of the set and end up feeling defeated. The energy to cultivate ourselves, to learn, and to share, is diminished against our will.

Perhaps we should decide to spend one evening a month doing something we enjoy. And if that involves some new way of organizing ourselves, would it not prove that we have not given up?

Time for sexuality

Making love depends not only on desire and energy. It takes time. A lot of it, if one is single and must budget time to seek and keep up one or more relationships. If one is married, a real sexual relationship cannot be achieved while fighting off sleep and trying not to wake the children.

And when the lovemaking is good, don't we have the fantasy or the impression that there is so much more to discover. Do we know how to give pleasure to our partner or do we lack the time to explore, to talk about it, so that these times acquire a special aura?

Do we know how to forget external demands to make ourselves truly available or, simply, to have a better knowledge of our body and its reactions?

Are we convinced that it is legitimate to set aside time for our sexuality?

Between the supermarket and far-off places

Time for consumption

One of the best ways to save money is to lack the time to spend it. Shopping is part of our modern amusements; it could even be considered one of its compensatory frenzies. But it can become as frustrating as bulimia. We buy without choosing just as we eat without pleasure only to fill ourselves, because we lack time.

Some managers find the time to buy socks only when they are on a business trip because that is the only time they have an hour to kill. Those who have children use their shopping time on the obligatory Saturday morning trips to the supermarket to fill up the refrigerator. When we do find time for some personal errands, we usually have a guilty conscience.

And when we do buy something, we lack the time to learn how to take advantage of it or even to learn how to use it. Consumption does not improve us the way culture does, but it relaxes us. The pleasure is diminished when we don't have enough time to devote to it, and our shopping becomes more and more sloppy since we don't have enough time to look and to compare. Welcome to shopping on the Web!

Time for travel

It takes time to travel, and that is good. Changing our locale guarantees time spent differently and elsewhere. As a bonus, there is the discovery and the knowledge of our world. A successful trip is like an active meditation. Without effort, for days on end we see things differently.

How many times have we come back from a trip having made a decision in an area of our life that had nothing to do with the place we visited? A simple change of location made possible a more direct access to our self. It is no accident that for several generations "tripping" was synonymous with taking drugs.

We travel when we are young when we have the means to do it. Then between the ages of twenty-five and forty we are caught up in responsibilities, and travel becomes more difficult. But we must try not to stop completely, if only because travel is therapeutic for a couple that is going through a difficult phase or in order to reestablish contact with one's children. The time to travel is worth the effort. How long has it been since you took a real trip?

Rest and reading

Time for resting

"I'll have time enough to rest when I am dead," an old family cook used to tell me when I was a child. If you are

among those now reading this book, you probably subscribe to this saying. I agree: life is so rich and interesting
and rest is not exciting. But—and remember the section on
"time and the body"—taking care of ourselves can make
the difference between pleasure and discomfort, between
optimism and depression.

Haven't we often been surprised to wake in a dreamy
mood after the first good night's sleep we have had in a
long time? Those who chase time forget that you cannot
get along without rest. Even a happy event is tiring. The
parents of a newborn are exhausted; the boss who has finished his accounts is bushed; the surgeon who has successfully transplanted a kidney is washed out; the newlyweds
are dying to go to sleep at the end of their happiest day.

If we underestimate the need to rest, we will miss many
of the best moments of our life.

Time for reading

Some insomniacs at least educate themselves. But if one
needs to sleep, when does one read in this life full of tension? We are ashamed of the skimmed newspapers and the
barely opened books we earnestly wanted to read. We
avert our eyes when we pass a bookstore for fear of rousing our regrets.

Nevertheless sometimes, full of hope and illusion, we
purchase the desired book and place it on our night table,
as if we could absorb it by osmosis during the night. And

when vacation time rolls around, the pile of unread books is there, ready to hop into the suitcase. With a little luck, some of those books will be read before we come back.

A personal question: this book, yes, the one you are holding at this moment, how long has it been since you bought it?

It has been said that reading is an "unpunished vice." Today its absence is a source of searing guilt.

What's even worse is that if during the day we manage to steal an hour of reading, we feel guilty as if we had something better to do. Hurray for public transportation! It is the one place we can read with an easy conscience.

To love and to give

Time to love

It has been said, once, that there is no love, but only proofs of love. It may be that time available is the greatest proof. What good are oaths if the lover is not present and assiduous? Chronic unavailability is not conducive to romantic relationships. Some women often think: "If you're seeing too much of a man, marry him!"

It is not enough to be together. The time for love comes when one is engaged in loving. We make love, we talk about it, we show our reverence for it in thousands of symbolic ways, we sacrifice at altars to show that this love exists. Not only do we have to find the time, but we have to nourish it with a very special attentiveness.

Is there room for love today in your life? Would there be more love if you had devoted a little more time to it? Mistakes are often due to a lack of experience.

When we are young, we think the magic of love will last. Then we find out that love is a plant that fades if it is not watered with time. Take up your watering cans!

Time for others

On some days, it seems that other people have conspired to take up all our time. Why even think of giving them more time? Of course, the others are not all the same. They may be those, such as family members, colleagues, and people with whom we are involved in a project, to whom we are duty-bound, and those we would like to see more often. Friendship is not in good health these days; it is rusting for lack of time. As in the case of travel, it is often sacrificed during the years we are overburdened. If we miss someone, it may still be possible to make an effort and renew a friendship.

The "others" are also the anonymous people about whom we are reminded only at times of tragedy or catastrophe, those who have had less luck than we because of their birth or other circumstance. It may not be possible for us to give them anything other than a check, especially if we are supporting a family. Nevertheless, it may be that a time for solidarity is as necessary to us as a time of love and of pleasure. "They" need it and perhaps we do too.

Playing as a family

Time for the family

Not everyone has a family, but those who do know that whether it is small or large, it gobbles up time. We have fewer children and we often live far from our parents, but family ties last longer because life expectancy is longer. We think odd thoughts: "How old will I be when my son retires?"

Many a woman finds herself around the age of fifty-five or sixty torn between her old mother who complains she doesn't see her enough, her daughter in a marital crisis, and her grandchildren who would like a full-time grandmother.

We are the most overburdened during the twenty-year period between the birth of our children and the time when we expect them to be on their own. During those long years, mothers feel stressed and fathers guilty though not as stressed. There is never enough time for the family and the time spent together is constantly negotiated because there would be nothing left for ourselves if we gave all that was asked for. There are no perfect solutions.

Time for playing

Regression is used in modern therapeutic techniques. Rebirthing, for instance, was a method based on respiration to help us to retrieve our earliest sensations. This extreme technique can sometimes blast away psychological blockages and early traumas.

It is possible to regress at leisure and for one's own good in a less radical way. When was the last time we played the buffoon or sang at the top of our lungs—without the help of alcohol—or acted dumb? The part of us that is child and animal has little opportunity to express itself after childhood. Don't we want to be taken seriously? Is that why we avoid showing that we could also not be serious?

The best way of regressing joyfully is to play with small children or animals, and not only to please our current partner. The most respected psychologists are currently rediscovering that adults need to play. Let us take the time to do it without feeling guilty.

Time for learning

It is good to continue learning during all of one's life, and not just in order to avoid the unemployment office. Continued learning has a significant antiaging effect. It is also good for our self-esteem to feel that we can still master the computer or learn a new language.

But few people learn Russian in order to keep their brain cells in shape or as a challenge. The investment in time is too great. It is difficult to keep on learning when you are leading an active life rich in connections with friends, family, and work.

Luckily, there is still the pleasure of pottery or watercolor or the piano. An activity in which we use our hands represents a radical change and forces us to commit to a specific time that provides us with an almost legitimate reason to attend to ourselves. Be sure to take advantage of such a hobby.

Time for creating

Our jobs are often too predictable and too repetitive. As the years pass and as we become better at them, the range of our activities runs the risk of contracting. It is important to prove to ourselves that we are not too specialized or too narrow. A regular life and family responsibilities can quickly enclose us.

Creativity in any field summons other aspects of ourselves. We should not stop writing, painting, drawing, or making objects when we stop going to school. With technological activities such as photography or videography we can capture other aspects of the world in which we live.

But creative time is very personal and is not easily accommodated by tight schedules. If we want time to create, we need to find places, internships, or competitions that allow us to concentrate in a dependable way. We will always have more to express than we have time for.

Meditation and spirituality

NOT LONG ago, we were told that the goal of meditation was to create or to find God. Withdrawing temporarily from others and engaging with our inner self were not encouraged. Oriental wisdom suggests meditation as another approach. No matter the form or the content of the meditation, it opens the doors to our interior self—a vast universe that remains to be explored.

It takes time, decades, to become aware that many essential answers are already within us. We have to wish it and we need the method and the time to find them, or rather to make ourselves vulnerable to them—thus the practice of some form of meditation that is not necessarily religious.

Lay spirituality will have a great future in the new century. This spirituality affirms only that questions about the meaning of life, the nature of beauty, and the presence of mystery exist in all of us. We need only place ourselves in propitious circumstances. Some need direct contact with beauty, nature, or human masterpieces. Others need only twenty minutes of Zen. But go find twenty minutes every day.

Time for solitude

FEW OF us would like to be hermits but who would not like to be a little bit alone?

Solitude now is looked down on and entire industries have been developed to allow us to flee it. Chosen solitude seems to some unattainable, to others forced solitude is a curse. Some find solitude at midnight, when the household is asleep. Others find it during business trips, in the quiet setting of a hotel room. But it is so easy to click on the television, to power up the laptop.

Solitude is not interrupted, only spoiled. A tête-à-tête with ourselves is not always welcome, but if it never takes place we will always remain ignorant of many things that concern us directly.

How do we arrange for a minimum of solitary time, that is, if we wish it? It is not easy to convince those around us that it is a necessity for us. To accept that our partner needs time without us is a sign of courtesy of the heart.

A very personal motivation

ALL THIS is very tempting, but isn't it only a dream? It is really too much! You are reading this book because you do not have enough time to do what you are already committed to, and here I am proposing an armful of new and even more remote goals. Is it pure perversity on my part?

On top of that, most people want to make better use of their time for professional reasons, and the projects I have discussed are of a personal nature. Is this reasonable? More reasonable than you think.

If we are to question our normal way of using our hours and weeks, we must first want to make a change. What can be more potent than the wish to live better and to enrich our personal life? Every effort to master time will necessarily have happy consequences for our life at work, but to get started, the promise of more personal pleasure will work better.

Here is the last of the most common objections: "You cannot plan your self the way you plan a business. In my personal life I require the unexpected, intuition, impulsivity."

How true! And how I regret almost daily that we do not live in a bucolic society in which our spontaneity has more opportunity to flourish!

But isn't it *because* we do not approach our personal goals in the same systematic spirit that the demands of our work take the lion's share of our life and we are left with only scraps of time?

We experience existential crises when our deepest needs are not met by the kind of life we are leading.

Why not throw our dreams the lifeline of a little bit of method?

A final confirmation: take a blank piece of paper and do "the last six months of your life" test. Imagine that you will suddenly disappear in six months while still in good health. What would you have liked to be sure of experiencing during these final months? You may think of new projects to add to your list and your priorities will have become even clearer.

How do the champions do it?

BEFORE YOU begin, take a look at some champions who have succeeded in reaching their goals.

A study carried out over fifteen years by the California psychologist Charles A. Garfield sought to understand what was different about "high-performance" individuals.

His subjects were people in the realm of sports, education, business, medicine, or the arts who performed significantly better and went further in their careers than did others. These people were not superhuman, but they did have a common approach to their problems, their goals, and their risks.

After examining the behavior of twelve hundred of these "achievers," Garfield found four characteristics they had in common:

1. They do what they do for the sake of "art," as a function of demanding internal goals.
2. They solve problems rather than look to blame others.
3. They mentally rehearse future actions and events.
4. They take risks confidently, after having considered worst-case scenarios.

It is important to note that they know when to stop working; they take vacations, avoid stress, do not allow themselves to be swamped by details, and they are masters at delegating.

Their use of the worst-case scenario technique allows them to reduce anxiety. Before undertaking a project, Garfield's achievers vision its failure and decide if they can live with it. Free from the fear of not succeeding, they can boldly pursue their project.

Garfield's findings confirm that it is not enough to formulate goals. We must learn to make them live in our head, to revise them, to look at them from every angle in order to anticipate both the satisfactions and the problems. *If we visit our goals ahead of time, our chances of reaching them and of benefiting from them are significantly improved.*

This technique of a "mental rehearsal of the future" is used by those who want to surpass themselves. Champions are trained to imagine intensely beating their own record and the feeling that then goes on within themselves. By living their performance ahead of time, they improve their chances of success. Now it's your turn!

WHAT I HAVE
LEARNED ABOUT TIME

*The confessions of a self-taught person · Glory or happiness? ·
Give time to time · I alone decide · No, not mine · A memo for
each idea · Reliability and the ill-bred · Stress, my sworn enemy
· My meeting with time · How do we begin? · My personal
account · A story about pebbles*

The confessions of a self-taught person

TIME HAS never been an abstraction for me; I don't know
why, but I felt early on that, no matter how long life would
be, it would pass quickly. I also understood that from
beginning to end it was important to stay in the best possible shape. Am I a perfectionist about time? Maybe, if we
judge by two rituals I have performed since my youth:

1. In order not to lose track of my days, I have been
   keeping a daily journal since the age of 17.

2. In order to keep going, I do 30 minutes of physical exercise every morning.

By performing these little rituals I am probably hoping to pacify our implacable master by making him a friend.

So, without false modesty but also without pretension, I will try in this chapter to recast these ideas and principles on the basis of my life, the only one I can talk about. For it is neither as philosopher nor as an organizational expert that I am competent to talk about time, but as a simple mortal. Like you, I found myself confronted by but unprepared for time. I realized right away that this was a fundamental problem. Rather than feeling anxious, I tried to do something about it.

Self-taught in the matter of time, it took me years to make any progress, to try various systems or attitudes, to perfect some tools, and then more years to coordinate these and to achieve some coherence. In the meantime, I compared my concerns and solutions with those of friends or acquaintances who were also pressed for time. I never stopped thinking about time.

Can it be said of someone that he is a perfectionist about life? If so, I would be delighted to accept this criticism because in my personal system (to each his own), life is the supreme value.

Not faith, not country, not equality, not order, and not even justice, but life, respect for life, the worship of life, the love of life, and therefore, not far behind, freedom.

Everything that disturbs, spoils, drains, reduces, or shortens life is abhorrent to me and I make every effort to avoid it. Thus the instinctive and profound care with which I try not to waste an iota of my time of life.

Glory or happiness?

As a journalist I meet many remarkable individuals. These writers, politicians, entrepreneurs, scientists, and philosophers have all followed unusual paths. I note with interest that their lives are balanced because they, like everyone, like you or me, have only twenty-four hours in their day.

Can they successfully maintain a balance between the different interests and pleasures in their lives: career, profession, family, creation, sensual pleasures, culture, travel, etc.?

I have come to the conclusion that if you want to be among the best in one area, lack of time forces you to accept a lower level of performance in many others.

The "grind" focuses entirely on his favorite sport, on his career, on his hobby, or on his children. I have seen artists who gradually cut themselves off from whatever is not their creation. I have spent time with politicians who put voters above their wives and children. I have worked with executives who spend half the year away from home. But I have also seen many women and men who value their family life so much that they put themselves out of the running in every other area—and especially in their work.

Every achievement is paid for by sacrifices. The high achievers make an essential choice that must be respected. But early on, life seemed to me too varied, too attractive to amputate any part of it. And so I wagered, perhaps unreasonably, that I could have it all, leaving out nothing.

I knew I would not be the first at anything, but I had the same idea as Mme de Stael: "Glory is the glittering mourning of happiness."

In order to maintain the equilibrium I prized, I had to learn to refuse a great deal and to measure beforehand the dose of life which each activity represented, from a dinner invitation (is it worth the hours of lost sleep?) to a new project (who will handle it? I? and at the expense of whom or what?).

To choose our time better, we have to know ourselves better, to be better informed on what life offers, and not to say yes too quickly.

Give time to time

"YOU HAVE to give time to time!" This hackneyed expression, usually repeated with a solemn air, simply means: "It is urgent to wait."

I would rather say it a little differently: to make a friend of time, it is best to treat it as a friend, that is, to devote some time to it.

In every life project, large or small, time is the least expensive element, but only if it is used well. The more we can predict and plan in peace, the better our projects will turn out. On the other hand, time lost at the beginning, through carelessness, is very expensive because in the process of catching up we will have to overcome obstacles.

Big businesses or nations can allow themselves these hemorrhages of time, but individuals with little money and only one life cannot do so—thus the importance of projects and goals. To create, launch, explore, learn, or build anything, you have to desire it, want it, and most of all, anticipate it. Since I have a limited supply of time, I am forced to mobilize it in advance if I want to use it in the best way possible.

Of course, I lose some spontaneity and heedlessness. I discussed this with people who say that at work they "can never predict," what will happen and with those who prefer to decide on a destination at the last minute and "always find something." I concluded that some of their trips were wonderful and some were disastrous. I prefer more regularity at the cost of a little investment in time, made at the right time.

Rather than do battle with time, I learned to get him on my side and win his support.

The better I can estimate in advance how much time an activity will take, the right moment for fitting it in, and its relationship to other goals, the more things happen they way I expect.

When my project begins to take shape, I feel a certain joy at having shaped it with the most precious raw material: time.

I alone decide

IF I let others decide how I use my time, I would be delegating my life to them. Certainly no one is completely free.

Every day we devote a block of eight to eleven hours, and sometimes even more, to the organization for which we work. How these hours are spent is to some degree controlled by others. When we work on an assembly line, none of that time is ours; even if we are a manager or in the "liberal" professions, or a director, less than half of our time is determined by us.

Nevertheless, many of those whose job is to make decisions allow their hours to be organized by their routines, their secretary, or their spouses. Are they perhaps looking to blame someone else for a life not to their taste?

Instinctively, I feel that surrendering the power of decision-making about my only irreplaceable resource is an abdication. In the Old West, cowboys signaled their independence by fondling the butt of the revolver at their hip. Myself, I carry my appointment book next to my heart; when I take off my jacket, I put it on my desk within reach.

This simple booklet registers all the transactions in the stock market of my life. Who other than I could trade them with full knowledge? Who, if not I, can tell if a visitor will be concise or wordy; if I will need to make a stop at home before leaving the office for a business trip; if a certain meeting will be important enough to require an hour of preparation; or if, after the meeting, I will have to call to verify a certain point?

If some businessperson tells me: "Let's do lunch. Our secretaries will arrange a date," I tell them to pass me their secretary for I am the only one to decide about my schedule. Many people seem to fear being in charge of organizing their lives.

A timetable should be chiseled rather than managed. It would make more sense to delegate one's checkbook than one's appointment book because our money is replaceable but not our time.

I am aware that this freedom is a luxury that only the self-employed can enjoy. Now that we have electronic appointment books that are managed collectively, it is the computer that decides when one's free time coincides with that of others and sets up a meeting. Clever, but enslaving.

No, not mine!

WHEN I still used to react to the demands of friends and colleagues and willingly gave away hourly slices of my days, a commercial for ice-cream cones caught my attention. It showed a little bear named Miko whose basket of cones was cleaned out by a forest of hands. He clutched the last one, wailing: "No! Not mine!" I have the same sense of anxious possessiveness about "my" hours.

We often write down in our appointment book only the meetings we have with others. This common error gives them a de facto priority in our allotment of time. Unless we are careful, we will soon find that we are running short of time for ourselves.

The important hours, those that make a difference, are precisely those when we are alone and can reflect, study, anticipate, even create. These are the most important hours, but we fail to set aside time for them in our appointment books. I took another step toward autonomy when I began to make regular appointments with myself at least once a week.

But to achieve autonomy and control over our future, it is not enough to keep an appointment book. We must also be sure not to forget anything that will help us execute our projects. In an abundant world, with fragmented activities, forgetting is a venial but enduring sin.

We forget first our own ideas, that cross our mind like butterflies and then fly away, if we do not have at hand the tools to capture them. We also forget the tasks we must accomplish and the commitments we have made. In general, the rate of forgetting increases as the square of overactivity.

But what we forget always takes its revenge and it catches up with us at the wrong moment in the form of loss of time, money, energy, or face.

Mastery of one's time begins with mastery over one's memory.

A memo for each idea

BECAUSE MY memory is not very reliable I had to find help. By chance, I inherited three things from my father: a pair of gold cufflinks, the love of dogs, and the habit of writing down ideas or things to do on small pads of paper. *These little cards of white paper are more precious to me than banknotes. I owe a great deal of my efficiency and peace of mind to them.*

In my left pocket I carry a little pad such as can be found in any stationery store. When I have an idea, I reach for a card. If someone asks me a question for which I don't have an answer, I write it down on a card. But only one item per card, which is thrown away when it has served its purpose or when the task has been accomplished.

Since I do not wear a jacket all the time, I put memo pads in every room, on the night table, in the bathroom, so I have no excuse for not writing down immediately what goes through my mind and remembering it at the right time, even if that time is six weeks away.

For example, if in six weeks I plan to go to London and I expect to need a copy of a contract, I write it down and date it for the eve of my departure. That day, I will take it out when I am getting my papers together for the trip.

How does the right card show up that day? Thanks to a standard-size cardboard folder with thirty-two compartments (one for each day, plus one for what goes beyond the month) that is found in all stationery stores and in which I arrange my cards by date. I call it my Memory because it relieves my memory of all these details and frees it up for what is important, creative, or pleasant.

Something as simple as the daily use of cards (sometimes I write a dozen a day) gives me a feeling of security that reinforces my self-confidence and also the confidence others have in me.

The system of cards is contagious because it is so simple. Those who live with me, as well as many of my collaborators, have begun to use it spontaneously. Every morning, my wife and I take care of practical details by exchanging cards, and after that we can then talk about more personal subjects.

Reliability and the ill-bred

RELIABILITY IS a key, if rare, element in the harmonious functioning of society and in our relations with friends and spouses. Those on whom you can count to "clean up," so to speak, are few and easy to spot. Obviously, they manage their time well.

It seems to me an individual becomes truly adult and mature only when others can begin to rely on him or her. If that is true, there are few adults.

What constitutes reliability? At a minimum, paying a little attention to others and following up on that attention. Business and government are full of subordinates who cannot reach their supervisors to talk or to sign a paper. Many individuals—who may not be that important—do not return phone calls, rarely answer letters, or do not follow through on an agreement until long after, if ever.

Though I hesitate to generalize, it seems to me that this sloppiness, this lack of good breeding and respect is less prevalent in Japan and in the United States than in Western Europe where we consider it a great courtesy if someone returns a phone call the same day.

Perhaps unfortunately, I feel myself bound by a promise, no matter how trivial, and have to find the means to fulfill my promises. In other words, I must allow enough time to do what someone has asked me to do and to arrange for the necessary reminders so that I do not forget. Here again, cards are invaluable to me.

Many people are unreliable not because they are ill-bred

but because they make appointments indiscriminately and find themselves swamped. They have so many contacts and obligations that they simply cannot live up to them.

Contrary to what most people think, it is much easier to say "no" than "yes."

A "yes" is already a commitment, an option on the future, an obligation. It is better to be parsimonious.

Saying "no" is unpleasant for a moment but the moment passes quickly, especially if it is said kindly and with tact. The other person is disappointed but more often than not understands. We like to say "yes" to please others and to get approval. But isn't that person more justified in resenting us if we say "yes" without following through than if we say "no" immediately and with a smile?

If we want to master our time, the little word "no" is the simplest and at the same time the must useful tool.

Stress, my sworn enemy

FOR A LONG time, busy people impressed me until I realized they were mostly stressed.

I detest stress and apparently I am not alone in this. In advanced countries, at least, stress is what most people currently complain about.

What I fear most about stress is not that it kills but that it keeps me from savoring life.

Why bother to work to acquire the amenities of life for ourselves and our loved ones if stress keeps us from enjoying them? In a cartoon I like, a woman in a restaurant suddenly tells her companion with dismay, " I just swallowed the caviar without noticing it."

As a young manager, it took me several years to realize that the essentials of life were passing me by (reflection, beauty, the sun, the taste of things, my children's childhoods), and that one could be productive without being stressed.

I realized that trying to do too many things in too little time was a sign of inexperience, disorganization and, often, insecurity. For example, because I was insecure, I did not yet know how much time to allot to a task. I therefore took the time to observe and measure, so that I could evaluate how long I spent on tasks.

My lack of organization spawned the classic errors: my desk was disorganized (the sight of its disorder drained my energy); my priorities were not clear and I had problems during the day knowing what I had accomplished; a tendency to do several things at once or the same thing several times; and a vague sense of following a twisted course.

I realized I had to stop reacting by trying to go even faster. On the contrary, I took care to say to myself, every time the motor began racing, "Stop and drop everything!" And so, little by little, I was able to slow down while still achieving good results.

It was at this point that I began to practice what has become the key element of my organization. Every day I have an "appointment with time" during which I plan the day so that I never lose its thread.

I began to glimpse "the" secret.

My meeting with time

A FOREST fire can be put out by a backfire. To fight the lack of time, I understood that I needed to devote time to think about the use of my time. By planning, I can think about it, shape it, and then choose what seems doable that day and that which is not.

Every morning, before breakfast, when no one can distract me, I live my day for the first time.

I take a special form, which I have designed. I call it my "day plan." This day plan is on blue paper, so I can find it easily on my desk. There are four columns: appointments, to do, phone calls, contacts. Each column is divided in small boxes. Then I take out of my Memory the papers filed for that day and sort them one by one and write down on my schedule all I need to do to accomplish the tasks scheduled for that day. Each small box lists something that I must do, such as a phone call or a communication with a coworker.

Then I check the messages on my answering machine and e-mail. I reply immediately to the most urgent and write down on my day plan those that can wait.

There, it's done! Everything I must do that day is written on this single form and is visually accessible. I keep it in front of me all day as a reminder of what has been scheduled until then. Needless to say, something unexpected always crops up. I cross out the box which has been accomplished and I write down the unexpected right away. I am thus able to see what I have done and what remains to be done.

Rarely is everything done by evening, but at least I am able throughout the day to choose what can wait until the next day. I remind myself that my goal is not to do more but to not feel stressed by over-commitment and by lack of organization. The next day I will write down what was not done, because I never use yesterday's schedule. Every day is new.

How do we begin?

IT IS possible to go even further with the key notion of spending time on time. Though less essential than the morning "meeting," a similar one in the evening provides an additional means of control. For, if we do not prepare adequately, we spend still less time reviewing after the fact. Nevertheless, such a review is a rapid and simple way of checking on ourselves. To review at the end of the day what really happened and why it happened is perhaps as important as trying to imagine it beforehand. Nothing happens entirely as we expect it to and we need to face up to normal ups and downs.

Here again there is nothing new under the sun. Five years before Jesus Christ, the Stoics practiced this retrospection; during air wars debriefing after a battle is as necessary as briefing beforehand. Comparing what really happened with what we had imagined is worth more than a hundred pages of theory about how we use time.

The principle of backfire is also useful in combating my periodic urges to procrastinate. I believe I am not the only person who finds it hard to face up to certain chores. Anything will serve as a pretext not to begin: getting a cup of coffee, reading the newspaper, making a phone call—in short delaying the plunge.

To fight the force of inertia, there is a Zen method that makes use precisely of inertia.

Do nothing, absolutely nothing. Remain seated with your hands on yours knees, eyes closed, empty your head as much as possible of thought and image except perhaps that of still waters, breathe deeply and quietly, and let waves of calm envelop you.

Keep this up until you feel really inert mentally and physically, then open your eyes slowly and immediately begin the task you were resisting.

My personal account

IN THIS chapter, since I have taken a more personal approach to time, I owe you an honest account of the way in which these principles and tools have changed my life.

* ❖ *I do not work less.* Without totally imitating my workaholic friends who say that "I find the forty-hour week such a good idea that I do it twice a week . . . ," I begin early and stay late. But I can honestly say that it is by conscious choice because I like what I do and it is a way of having fun. I could have more leisure time, but I have deliberately chosen not to do so.

❖ *I concentrate on the essential.* This, to me, is the most important choice I have made. I am conscious at every moment of the best possible use of my time and rarely feel that I am wasting it. I find the time to do what is important to me, and I refuse to do anything else.

❖ *I am not stressed.* I once took a *Time* magazine test on predispositions to stress. On a scale on which 30 indicates vulnerability and 50 is considered serious, my score was 6, which confirmed that one can be active without becoming frenetic.

❖ *I capitalize on life.* Even if I do not have a lot of "free time," I savor each hour of my private life. I have learned to anticipate my day with pleasure (starting with breakfast), and to live every hour with my mind free of "problems," since I know I will be able to take care of them during the hours set aside for them.

❖ *I need to make progress.* I am not a master of time, merely a student. Now that I have tasted the rewards of a more supple time, I measure the distance I still have to go. So I try, by reading and by practice, to find the key to progress by means of improved concentration and reflection. And that is thrilling.

A story about pebbles

I WILL end with a little parable that involves a demonstration of time management by an American professor. The professor fills a pail one by one with a dozen big pebbles and asks his students: "Is the pail full?" "Yes," the students answer. "Are you sure?" He takes out a bag of gravel and empties it into the pail. "And now, is the pail full?" "Maybe," say the students who are now more careful. The professor then takes a container of sand, shakes the pail so that the stones rearrange themselves, and empties the sand into the pail. "Now is it full?" "No!" shout the students. The professor then empties a big bottle of water into the pail until the liquid reaches the rim. He then asks the class: "What is the point of this demonstration?" A student raises his hand: "It is to show that even if you think your schedule is full you can still add to it." No," answers the professor, "I only wanted to remind you that unless you put your big stones in first, you will never be able to put them in later."

What are the "big stones" of your life? Your loved ones? Your career? Your personal development? Creative work? Having more fun? Achieving an understanding of what you are doing on Earth?

Whatever they are, it is up to you to make sure that they take a prominent place in your time. Now you know a little more about how to do it.

It is your turn now! Good luck!

YOUR TIME IN THE NEW CENTURY

A change of time? · *We will live a long life* · *Urgency and tension*
· *Attached to our cell phone* · *Ubiquity and nomadism* · *Glued to
the screen* · *Time flies on the Internet* · *The war over time* · *The
young set the trend* · *Surviving modernity*

A change of time?

IS IT because we are attracted by round numbers or excited by changing centuries and millennia, that we have heard and read about so much nonsense about the turning of the new millennium?

Well, here we are at last. What has changed? Nothing, of course, in the nature of time, which remains as immutable as at creation. Nor has anything changed in our attitudes toward the passage and the use of time, which remain individual and depend on our temperament and the course our life takes. Now you know that to change them you will need to make an effort and . . . some time.

On the other hand, the beginning of the millennium coincides with the spread of scientific discoveries and technologies that are having a major impact on the course of our life and on our time. Let us look at the way these changes will affect our way of life in light of what we have discussed in this book.

The most important recent discoveries have been not in telecommunications but in biology, resulting in a longer life expectancies. The phases of our life on earth will be rearranged and we will have to deal with new questions.

The other discoveries are a result of the more or less sophisticated combination of increasingly powerful electronic chips and increasingly effective communications networks. Let us not call it information technology, even if the computer has now become our permanent partner. Put simply, there will be chips everywhere, in all the objects of our daily life, and we will connect to the Internet as frequently as we reach for a tissue.

Some powerful trends are already evident:

- ❖ a sense of urgency and an increase in tension
- ❖ an emphasis on the immediate and on improvisation
- ❖ ubiquity and wandering
- ❖ an addiction to the screen
- ❖ networks of tribes
- ❖ social stratification on the basis of technical competencies

Technology does not save you time at first; it may even take up more time than it saves. But it has become imperative that we integrate it into our lives. How do we do it without becoming increasingly stressed?

We will live a long life

MY FRIEND Charles turned fifty-seven at the beginning of the new century. Because of an unexpected event in his professional life, he was able to retire early and he loves it. Since he is in good health, statistically he has another thirty years to live—more than half of the time he has already lived. His children are grown, his grandchildren do not live with him, and his fifty-year-old wife expects to work another ten years. He will have to invent another life for himself and he admitted to me that he had not really thought about it.

In the last hundred years our life expectancy has doubled and it continues to increase by two months every year. Even if we do not reach a hundred, we can remain alert far into old age. We now speak of the –10 effect (fifty-year-olds look forty, seventy-year-olds look sixty) and many now expect the –15 effect.

Even without considering the economic upheavals caused by the additional years of retirement, all our clichés about old age have been shattered.

In the United States, 80 percent of baby boomers now more than fifty years old state that they want to work after sixty while today only 12 percent of the sixty-year-olds are in fact working, and a quarter of the fifty-year-olds claim they want to work to maintain their salary, but a third wants to continue working "for fun." Since there will not be enough work for everyone of them, they will have to create their own activities. As in the case of my friend Charles, they probably have not even thought about it.

Just as the Dutch reclaimed land from the sea, we are reclaiming from time a new period of our life, and we have not yet assimilated the opportunities and demands the new segment of time will make. To live longer and remain young, isn't that the realization of an ancestral dream? And yet we are not ready for it.

Having lived two-thirds of our life in a state of stressful hyperactivity, will we be able to enter a time as limp as a sail when there is no wind?

It is a mistake to think that we will be able to think about it "when the time comes." We risk depression and illness if we suddenly change our speed. The prospect of a long retirement period is another reason to strengthen the time we devote to ourselves while we are in the prime of life because we will have to build our life on those personal activities during those years reclaimed from time.

Urgency and tension

In a large European electronic company, I have seen executives classifying their memos a "top urgent," "very urgent," and merely "urgent." "Important" did not even exist for them as a category. Our tendency to privilege urgency is increasing for three reasons:

- ❖ Globalization and unemployment, which together have increased competition. We have to stay ahead of those who sell the same products as we or those who could replace us in the work force. There is no question of letting up, even less of relaxing. The most fashionable business known as the Internet becomes a reference point. Those working in the Internet world count in "dog years." Everything moves so quickly that, as in the lives of our favorite quadrupeds, one year counts as seven. In this atmosphere, how can we afford not to drive ourselves forward?
- ❖ Telecommunication, which facilitates and accelerates the exchange of messages. Surveys of the employees of some of the largest businesses in the world have established that each one of us receives each day on average 178 messages or documents. Choosing, dealing with, classifying, and answering them increases the stress on us in proportion to the excess of information.

At the same time, cell phones and e-mail have transformed communication into a game of ping-pong. The immediacy of the e-mail message creates the impression that an answer cannot wait. Customers have become less willing to wait for answers. It is unacceptable to wait more than twenty-four hours to respond to an e-mail. Urgency has become the norm.

For the last fifteen years the demand for increased productivity has been rising. In 1984, 20 percent of the salaried work force in France had to meet daily production quotas; at the end of the century, the proportion is 50 percent. Management is pressuring employees to produce more rather than hire more people. The employees must therefore work faster, so that again we have begun talking about stress at work.

Whatever the technological progress of the last century, we can see that the most effective use of our time is at stake for each of us. Speed is part of our culture. We have to deal with it and not allow it to create a sense of urgency and therefore of stress. The most astonishing technologies are only part of our path through life; the essential comes from the attitude of those who make use of the technologies.

Attached to our cell phone

THE CELL phone is becoming the handgun of the modern citizen. It is being adopted more rapidly than were earlier technologies such as the telephone, the television, the VCR, and the computer. Soon, the majority of the population will carry on his or her person this magic wand of communication.

The desirability of this instrument can be explained only by the fact that it meets profound needs: we yearn for more freedom even as we yearn for closer relationships; and we seek the security of a cell phone because it assures us that we are never alone, that we are part of a network wherever we go.

Our relationship with time is also affected. We think ahead less and less. Young people especially, for whom the cell phone has become a prosthesis, an extension of the self, do not think ahead. Why bother writing down the number of the apartment where they are to dine when a phone call in front of the door will do? More and more we make dates at the last minute. The people in the group know they can reach each other instantly and that they can decide to order a pizza when everyone has assembled.

We are increasingly unable to wait. When someone is late for a meeting, we call for his cell phone number. Every delay caused by traffic or in a waiting room is immediately put to use by calling someone. Without our knowing it, making contact becomes more important than thinking.

Immediacy and improvisation take precedence over planning and organization. In video games the person who shoots the quickest scores. If you take time to think, you have already lost. The illusion of omnipotence is created when a simple click of the mouse can send an order to the stock exchange to buy or sell at the other end of the world.

The model of the chess master is replaced by the model of the fastest draw.

Clearly, this frenzy changes nothing about the absolute necessity to think strategically about one's life and actions. It actually increases the advantage of those who take the time to think. They need only an extra dose of moral strength to avoid getting caught up in the stampede. In any case, they have learned to use the new instruments to their advantage. Like written messages of all kinds, answering machines and message centers allow them to decide when to respond. When you can see the telephone number of the caller on your screen, you can choose whether or not to answer. Deferred communication thus becomes a tool to be used skillfully. Once again, the new technologies are not harmful in themselves if you take the time to think about the best way to use them.

Ubiquity and nomadism

WHEREVER I go I take along my laptop and my cell phone. Together they are responsible for my electronic mail and even my faxes. My wife prefers to carry in her purse a high-capacity diskette that contains her work in progress and her favorite programs because she finds her computer too heavy. When she goes to the country or returns to Paris, she slips this portable memory into her computer and resumes her work. Each in our own way, we are never cut off from our work. Should we be congratulating ourselves?

Not only is collaboration with distant colleagues now possible, but work itself has also become portable. We imagine globetrotters who are in Caracas one day and Stockholm the next, but, closer to home, like nomads, we carry our work on our laptops with us wherever we go. It is practical but also alienating.

I pointed out earlier that professional time does not differ in nature from personal time. Modern technologies make this unity visible. There is a greater risk now that the professional will end up devouring the personal. But, in the same way, my most personal communications, written or oral, can reach me at work. And that is nothing in comparison to what we are promised in the near future. Cell phones with 1,000 programmed addresses will replace our address book and will run Internet applications. Our files and archives will reside in a server that can be searched from anywhere in the world. We will be able to access the server from any machine just as we can now telephone from anywhere.

In the same way that we are no longer cut off from those who are important to us, we will remain in contact with all our work documents, even in the middle of the desert, if we are crazy enough, thanks to communications satellites. Now the web in which we are both the spider and the fly surrounds us completely. I hear you exclaim: "How horrible! Not that!" Think again!

So often I have been grateful for these tools because they allowed me to stay in the country another day or another week while continuing to work. I can leave the city earlier on the weekend, knowing that where I go I will receive the document I would have had, previously, to wait for at work.

We always return to the issue of the management of time.

We are indeed to be pitied if we allow machines to dictate to us! But if we make good use of their potential in the framework of our hygiene of time, what good fortune!

Glued to the screen

MY NEW laptop is equipped with a DVD reader, those disks the size of CD that hold an entire movie and have impeccable transmission. It is now possible for me to begin my day by checking my electronic messages on this machine and to end it with the same machine watching a Woody Allen movie. In between I will have written, transmitted, searched for information, found archival material, printed recipes, checked the weather, listened to the radio, and reserved tickets for the theater, all on this computer the size and shape of an art book.

No, I am not a computer addict. Until five years ago I had never even used a computer. But you become addicted to it once you begin. Everything, or almost everything, can now take place on the screen that thus becomes an extension of our self. It is not yet true for everyone, even in the developed nations, but it will happen very soon for a simple reason: the fusion of the roles played by the computer screen and the television screen.

We can already watch movies and programs on a computer, and more and more we will receive our e-mail, surf the Web, and make our purchases on the television screen in the living room. Almost without our knowing it, during the last ten years, information technology and television have begun to talk the same numerical language.

All modes of information transfer—writing, speech, images—now use the code that translates everything into ones and zeros. Everything can be transposed and retransmitted easily on all the screens of our life. Thirty years ago we complained that we were glued to the screen three hours a day, but it was mostly in the evening, for fun. Now it will be all day and for most of what we do during our waking hours. Is this a science fiction nightmare? It is certainly not science fiction; we have reached the point at which we take it for granted. A nightmare? We could say no if only we were not so dependent on it.

The gains in time are clear since many delays have been eliminated. *Now we can do at home many of the things, including work, that in the past were done elsewhere.*

And if we add the things we can now do easily, such as buying products from another country, it is extraordinary how much more is possible. The dangers are just as clear: the psychological difficulty in going from the virtual bubble to the real; the confinement with a machine; the impoverishment of our direct relationships; and fewer and fewer reasons to leave home. Do I need to repeat that, as in the case of all contemporary diversions, personal counter-strategies are essential as well as possible in order to preserve our vitality and our interior life?

Time flies on the Internet

THE INTERNET shows us the world of the future. Agreed! But are we gaining time or losing it?

The first hemorrhage of time takes place when we try to access the Internet. Most of us still reach it through telephone lines, but you might as well eat your mashed potatoes with a straw. While you wait for a Web site to appear on the screen, you lose precious minutes because the sites are often illustrated in rich graphics that take a long time to load. And in order to make intelligent use of the Web, you often have to go from link to link before finding the right site. Internet service providers will solve this problem by creating specialized high speed networks. Many offices already use them. But we will have to wait another two years to do it easily and affordably at home.

We also lose time because so much is available on the Web. Millions of sites already exist and thousands more come into being every day. It is more than probable that the site we need already exists. But how do you find it? Computer scientists are working to create more powerful and complex search engines. But at this point you rarely find what you need right away. To become adept at searching, you need flexibility and practice; without these you only scratch the surface of this fertile terrain.

It is easy to become addicted to the Web. Each site points to others that can be reached with a click, and there you find other links and other possibilities or paths. It seems like magic, and because it is fun to find sites that were unknown and unexpected until that moment, you can spend hours skipping around electronically. We realize that here too we will have to acquire mastery in a field in which knowledge is passed along from one person to another.

Many are discouraged by the growing pains of this young system. "I don't have the time to search the Web." But everything will happen so quickly—from the capacity of the "pipes" to the flexibility and the precision of searches, as well as our own training. So let us not get discouraged too quickly. The tool is worthwhile, but we cannot avoid the learning curve.

The war over time

PRIMITIVE HUMANITY fought a war over fire; there were wars over women, gold, land, provinces, and then continents. And let us not forget the wars we are still fighting over oil and water. The social controversies of the last century were first about money and then about its just distribution. There have not been any major strikes over time, but sometimes those in charge found it cheaper to reduce the hours or days of work rather than to raise salaries. At the beginning of the twenty-first century inflation has thus far been held in check, and workers prefer more free time to salary increases.

Now that telecommuting makes gray matter (the principal raw material of modern production) available anywhere, fixed schedules seem absurd to the manager whereas to the employee—who is paid less well—safeguarding his family life has become his hobby-horse. However, these same workers, when they rest during the weekend, enjoy being able to do their errands when it suits them and want the stores to be open when they are free.

In the war over time, those who want more free time will face those who want to choose when they work, 7 days out of 7 and 24 hours out of 24. There is a growing need now for automated systems, such as automatic teller machines, that serve without human intervention. But a machine that dispenses drinks, even hot drinks, has not yet replaced the atmosphere of a coffeehouse.

The young set the trend

THE WAR over time will renew the traditional divisions between the educated and well-equipped elite and the rest of humanity. The use of sophisticated computers and other digital tools demands a real, new education. On the planet, two groups of people risk being left out: those who don't know how to use computers, and those who do not speak English and therefore have limited ability to use the Internet. And then of course there are those who do not have access to up-to-date computers. The privileged always have had more time, and that becomes truer every day.

The more technology invades the way we work and amuse ourselves, the more the social pyramid becomes inverted. In ancient or primitive civilizations in which techniques did not change, those who had the most experience played the most important part and were in charge. From now on, the skilled adolescent, who on his own is able to create his own Web site or an illustrated presentation by importing images from around the world, gives the most educated professors an inferiority complex. Even if our developed societies are getting older, today the acceleration of technology allows the young to set the tone.

The introduction of the Internet has added a new cultural dimension. The machines are easy to use and will become more so. What is difficult, on the other hand, is learning a new language, a new way of searching for and using knowledge. Finding something on the Internet is only partly a rational procedure. You also need a dose of instinct, shrewdness, patience, and luck. Those who are born with it will adapt with ease; others will have to undergo a real apprenticeship that will test mercilessly their capacity for adaptation.

As our life expectancy increases, so does the risk that we will die as ignoramuses. Many sixty-year-olds have caught on, and the first thing they do when they retire is buy a computer. If they are lucky, their grandchildren will teach them how to use it and it will become a way of establishing unexpected and lasting ties.

The new millennium can play its full symbolic role by encouraging those who are still fearful to become acquainted as soon as possible with cybercommunication, if they are to keep from feeling old before their arteries are.

Surviving modernity

EVEN IF technology is the source of novelty and excitement at the beginning of this century, we must not allow it to turn our heads. To make better use of our time and to live better, no machine is more useful than good sense. So as not to lose more time than I gain from progress and without refusing to make use of progress, I try to obey three simple principles:

❖ I try to maintain compatibility among my electronic tools. I know more than one person who uses a Mac at home and an incompatible PC at work. If on top of the computer they also have a pocket electronic organizer that performs some of the same functions as the other two, they are always asking themselves where they have left the document they are working on. In any case, we use only a fraction of the capacity of these marvelous machines. Let us buy the simplest and let us try to stick to only one system.

❖ I wait until technology has improved. The manufacturers of electronic equipment are constantly changing their products. As soon as you have purchased the most modern machine, you read that there is a "new, updated" version without which you cannot live. The advice of competent people will help you identify those that will be helpful to you. Real improvements come from the power, speed, and the number of hours you can use your laptop or cell phone without recharging, and, most of all, from the speed of connection to the network. As for more sophisticated programs, it is best to wait until several users have assured you that they have become indispensable. If the operation of a machine seems too complicated, you can be sure that the creator or editor will soon come out with a more user-friendly version. Tomorrow will be even simpler.

❖ I know when to remain manual. If some of your procedures work fine in a manual mode, nothing compels you to adopt an electronic version.

For example, I tested the Palm type organizers that allow you to keep addresses and to record meetings. When

I used it, I found that it was a great improvement over an address book, but that my appointment book and a pencil were a simpler, quicker, and more practical way to write down my appointments and visualize the use of my time.

It is best to follow the simple principle that if you are not organized, these machines will only add to your confusion. On the other hand, if you have some control over your time, you will love using them. Have fun!

CONCLUSION

The Art of Time

THE GREEKS were the first people to theorize about art. They were looking for the meaning and the rules for those rare human creations that allow us to develop our inner coherence. They concluded that five elements were necessary in art: order, equilibrium, contrast, unity, and harmony.

Our technical civilization has not improved on this theory. In fact, aren't these rules the expression of our own yearnings and sources of satisfaction? They are as applicable to us as they are to the friezes of the Parthenon.

If the expression "the art of time" is not a gratuitous formula, it is because these five attributes can be applied to time and be made part of our own work.

- *Order*, because we need to know where our time goes. It is hard for us to grasp time in its entirety, but we can allocate it and organize it rationally. There is less confusion once the structures we haven chosen are in place and show themselves to be enduring.
- *Equilibrium*, when we discover that allowing our time to be swallowed up in one dominant activity, no matter how satisfying, leads to atrophy and disconnection elsewhere. Scarce time is necessarily rationed between the poles of our lives and it is we who decide the distribution. We will be the first to suffer the consequences of an unbalanced distribution.
- *Contrast*, when we accept ourselves as we are, that is, as creatures who do not tolerate doing the same thing for long. We need to learn to alternate the intellectual and the physical, concentration and diversion, solitude and conviviality, action and withdrawal. This never-ending movement constitutes the dance of life. And is not dancing one of the most lively arts?
- *Unity*, because order is not compartmentalization but the emergence of a number of perspectives that allow us to comprehend the whole. Segmenting our time would mean losing the unexpected syntheses, the fertile resonances that life offers us. Modern time seems atomized. Only we, through inner discipline, can confer unity on it.

❖ *Harmony* in Greek meant "together." Of course it follows from the preceding four attributes. You cannot define it, you can only feel it. In the morning we ask ourselves: "Does the day look as if it is going to be a good one?" and in the evening: "Did I use my time well?" Harmony is at once the test and the reward of our mastery.

The art of time thus seems to be the first step toward an art of living that, in addition to what we have just said, allows us to accomplish our projects. When we arrive at even an average mastery of time, we have a far greater chance of bringing our projects to fruition.

At first it seems the discipline needed to achieve mastery of time seems constraining, but that is only a stage, and it is so worthwhile! Isn't a more harmonious and more productive time one of the most precious and beautiful gifts we can give ourselves?

Let us use once again the comparison with dieting we made earlier: at first, every regimen seems difficult. Every meal is a test of willpower, but the day comes when the forbidden food no longer tempts us. It is no longer a question of diet but of new eating habits.

The goal of the advice given in this book is ostensibly to help us make better use of our days and our weeks. But my real goal is to help us internalize the form, the flow, and the value of our time.

When that is accomplished, we will look at how every element of our life fits in and weighs on our time. When that happens, we will no longer need a method. It will have allowed us to reach a new level of awareness. We can now discard it by the road like a vehicle that brought us to the right destination.

We will continue our progress toward mastery according to our own pace, because the need to master time never disappears.

As long as we have time left to live.

About the Author

JEAN-LOUIS SERVAN-SCHREIBER is a leading French journalist and media executive. The founder and former chairman of Groupe Expansion—publisher of *L'Expansion,* France's leading business magazine—and the author of six books, he is now the editor and publisher of the monthly magazine *Psychologies.* He taught journalism at Stanford University in 1971. He lives in Paris.